Catechetical Instruction
and the
Catholic Faithful

Catechetical Instruction and the Catholic Faithful

Edited by
MSGR. GEORGE A. KELLY

Introduction by
SILVIO CARDINAL ODDI
Prefect, Sacred Congregation for the Clergy

ST. PAUL EDITIONS

NIHIL OBSTAT:
   Rev. Richard V. Lawlor, S.J.

IMPRIMATUR:
   ✠ Humberto Cardinal Medeiros
   Archbishop of Boston

ISBN 0-8198-1418-0 (cloth)
      0-8198-1419-9 (paper)

Copyright © 1982, by the Daughters of St. Paul

Printed in the U.S.A. by the Daughters of St. Paul
50 St. Paul's Ave., Jamaica Plain, Boston, MA 02130

The Daughters of St. Paul are an international congregation of religious women serving the Church with the communications media.

CONTENTS

Introduction
    JESUS CHRIST IS THE MESSAGE
        Cardinal Silvio Oddi
        Prefect of the Sacred Congregation
        for the Clergy............................. 13

Chapter One
    A PASTORAL VIEW OF CATECHETICS
        Most Rev. Anthony J. Bevilacqua, J.C.D., J.D.
        Auxiliary Bishop-Chancellor
        of the Diocese of Brooklyn 37

Chapter Two
    MORAL EDUCATION: A COMPARISON
    OF SECULAR AND RELIGIOUS MODELS
        Paul C. Vitz
        New York University....................... 89

Chapter Three
    CATECHIZING THE POOR
        Sr. Michelle McKeon, S.C.
        Saints Peter and Paul Parish, South Bronx 138

Chapter Four
    CATECHESIS FOR ADULTS
        Sr. Theresa Catherine Shea, O.P.
        Molloy College, Rockville Centre,
        New York 150

Chapter Five
> THE CONTENT OF CATECHESIS
> Most Rev. Austin B. Vaughan, S.T.D.
> Episcopal Vicar
> Archdiocese of New York 160

Chapter Six
> WHO IS GOING TO SEE TO IT
> THAT YOUNG CATHOLICS ARE TAUGHT
> WHAT IT MEANS TO BE A GOOD CATHOLIC?
> Rev. Msgr. George A. Kelly, Director
> Institute for Advanced Studies
>   in Catholic Doctrine
> St John's University, New York 185

Chapter Seven
> CONTEMPORARY CATECHESIS
> IN THE UNITED STATES:
> STATE OF THE QUESTION
> Rev. Msgr. George A. Kelly 214

Index 225

INTRODUCTION

Jesus Christ Is the Message

Cardinal Silvio Oddi
Prefect of the Sacred Congregation for the Clergy

It is a joy for me to come to St. John's University to share in your celebration of the second anniversary of the publication of Pope John Paul II's Apostolic Exhortation *Catechesi tradendae,* one of the great pastoral documents of our times. My pleasure is, in fact, double, because, not only is it a satisfaction for me as Prefect for the Sacred Congregation for the Clergy, which looks after the catechetical apostolate in the universal Church, to carry out one of my duties, but it is also a delight to be part of this Symposium which is one of the events designated to mark the four hundredth anniversary of the birth of Saint Vincent de Paul, the Founder of the Congregation of the Mission. The Vincentians have always been dear to my heart, not only because of their long and impressive service to the Church, particularly in the formation of the clergy and in teaching the Gospel to the poor, but also because I had the good fortune to be associated closely with them early in my priestly life. My first diplomatic superior was a Vincentian, and today I reside in one of their houses in Rome. So, even though I have just flown the Atlantic, here at St. John's I feel that I have scarcely left home.

Religious Freedom in America

I believe that almost everyone who comes to the United States from abroad to speak about religion must feel at ease because of your tradition of religious freedom. Your legislatures make laws about taxes, health and speed limits, but never touch religion. So here in the United States one can speak the truth as God gives one to know the truth without fear or pressure. What a great and enviable blessing you have received from your founding fathers. But what great responsibility you also have before God to use your freedom well, for freedom has its limits and its limits are the objective truth.

From the earliest days of your country's history, Catholics enjoyed the same rights as the followers of other religions. The early struggle of the Catholic Church in the United States for survival was not due to official persecution but principally to a grave shortage of priests. Most of your early co-religionists spoke English, of course, but there were few priests in the whole world at that time who did so, and most of these, for one reason or another, were thought to be needed where they were. French-speaking priests had come to the New World as missioners and they drifted down from Canada to help nourish your young and growing Church, but few of them spoke English well enough to provide easy religious formation of the young.

Second Solution

Your religious forebears could have reacted in two ways to this difficult situation: they could have simply neglected to give any religious training to their children, or the laity itself could have stepped in to substitute for the absent clergy, to whom most catechesis in Europe was normally entrusted at that time. You chose the second solution, and your lay men and lay women responded so well that, from a small scattered Church in a new country, there emerged a numerous and vigorous priesthood, an enormous and fervent sisterhood and brotherhood and a zealously apostolic laity, so much so that, only six score years after the establishment of your first diocese of Baltimore, American Catholics were already sending their own sons and daughters to fields afar, as missioners to needy, distant Churches.

The accomplishments of your early lay catechists are all the more remarkable when one reflects that, while you did enjoy religious freedom, the price you had to pay was a public school system in which religion could not officially be taught. How did you surmount that obstacle? From the very beginning you developed your own school system, so early in fact that the woman chiefly responsible for it danced at a birthday ball of the Father of your country, and before St. Elizabeth Seton died, a chain of Catholic schools had already begun to spread all across your land.

Some of your children, however, did not manage to attend these new parochial schools, and that is true even today. As a matter of fact, my beloved predecessor, John Cardinal Wright, enjoyed recalling, with a twinkle in his eye, that he never put foot as a student in a Boston parish school. He explained that he learned his prayers from his parents, his doctrine from the local pastor as well as from a devout Protestant teacher in the local public school, who took it upon herself to drill him in the *Baltimore Catechism*, which at that time was not on the index of prohibited books! The great Cardinal was fond of saying that his higher theological studies never succeeded in opening to him much more about the mystery of the Triune God than he learned from that remarkable Protestant lady in Boston, namely, that there are Three Persons in One God.

Your early Bishops had quickly seen the need for a reliable, complete summary of the doctrine of the Faith, to be used in teaching the faith in so heterogeneous and mushrooming a Church. As great tides of immigrants rolled across the Atlantic, Poles and Italians, Irish and

Germans mixed with Spanish and French and English, as well as with your growing Black population. All these had to be nourished in the same Faith, through religion teachers often as varied in culture and preparation as the catechumens themselves: immigrant mothers who knew little English, Protestant converts from Harvard, dedicated but unschooled religious, sisters with university training, learned priests, and some not so learned. Who can deny that the *Baltimore Catechism* was a major instrument in preserving the purity and the integrity of the Faith in the United States in circumstances which might easily otherwise have splintered the young Church into at least as many sects as there are States in your Union?

Warm Acceptance of Encyclical

Having been blessed with generous, devoted catechists from the first years of your history, and having produced a dependable resumé of the doctrine of the Faith, you did not find it too demanding a challenge to respond swiftly and effectively to Pope St. Pius X's call in 1905 for the establishment of the Confraternity of Christian Doctrine. Under the dynamic leadership of Archbishop Edwin V. O'Hara, the CCD eventually spread into every corner of your vast land and proved so vigorous and so apostolic that, under the inspiration of Archbishop Robert Lucey, the American Confraternity of Christian Doctrine became the spark that re-ignited the catechetical apostolate in Latin America at the middle of this century. Recently, the United States has become one of the first countries in the world to produce its own National Catechetical Directory, *Sharing the Light of Faith*, in accordance with the guidelines of the *General Catechetical Directory*, which was issued by the Congregation for the Clergy in 1969.

So, without doubt, you Americans have used your freedom well up until the present. You have not only known how to discuss catechetics but to do catechesis. In the true spirit of your country, external obstacles have not stopped your progress in the field of catechetics and religious education, for you have seen impediments not as roadblocks, but as stimulants to advance.

It is not surprising, then, that *Catechesi tradendae* has been so warmly received in the United States, as it was in the rest of the world, and that you have wanted to commemorate the second anniversary of its appearance with this Symposium. You have instinctively recognized that this apostolic exhortation of Pope John Paul reflects many positive aspects of the American catechetical movement, and offers a number of practical cautions to alert modern catechists to pitfalls they will inevitably run across in their efforts to nurture the Word of God in tender hearts living in a hostile world.

I believe there are three main reasons why *Catechesi tradendae* has made so favorable an impression in the United States.

Timely, Balanced and Practical

1) It is timely. It is obviously urgent to intensify religious formation at this moment of the Church's history, when so many religious indicators show a dramatic falling off, and sins against humanity are on the rise. For example: while murder, abortion, divorce and other attacks on man increase, sacramental confession has declined. While the Catholic population continues to grow, the number of vocations to the priesthood and the religious life has dropped; while theological controversies about fundamentals abound, the attendance at Sunday Mass falls. Certainly, a fresh look at religious formation is needed in our times.

2) It is a balanced document. The deposit of Faith and the values of Church tradition are effectively and happily defended, but, at the same time, the Church is presented as the guardian of a living tradition which must not reject the valid discoveries of natural science and must courageously examine their possible relation to

revealed truth, particularly in areas in which these meet in the Catholic conscience.¹

3) It is a practical document. *Catechesi tradendae* was not conceived spontaneously by either Pope Paul VI, who began it, nor by Pope John Paul II who produced it. Its origin was the Bishops' Synod of 1977. Virtually every point made in the exhortation, both positive and negative, has its source in that Synod, the aim of which was to treat the pastoral problems of today's catechetical apostolate, and which furnished a forum for the Bishops of the world to express their ideas. All the observations made by the Bishops were not, of course, of equal value, so it fell to the Holy Father to select, to cull, to fill in, to stress, to warn. The present document, then, could hardly be more practical, based as it is on the living experience of the universal Church. The Pope has, in his turn, sifted the wheat from the chaff, assembled a cohesive, responsive, up-to-date set of catechetical norms for the guidance of the entire Church; in a word, he has, once again, "confirmed the brethren" (Lk. 22:32).

Jesus Christ Is the Message

The core around which Pope John Paul II chose to fashion *Catechesi tradendae* is not only theologically impeccable but eminently apropos to the present catechetical moment. As you well know, the core of the document is Jesus Christ. Jesus Christ is the message. Notice carefully that the Pope does not juxtapose the *teaching* of Christ to the *spirit* of Christ, nor the historical Christ to the Christ of faith. The Pope speaks simply of Jesus Christ, the Word from the beginning (Jn. 1:1), the Word made flesh (Jn. 1:14), the Son of the Father (Mt. 17:5). The Pope talks both about things Christ said and things He did, because the Gospels recount both the words and deeds of Jesus. Jesus is not to be divided, as Saint Paul cautioned (1 Cor. 1:13), and that is why Pope John Paul does not restrict his comments to certain verbal teachings of Jesus, but refers also to His example, who He was, how He lived. Many of the Pope's remarks might be considered overly fundamental by some, until one realizes that not a few of today's attacks on the Church are going for the jugular, the very fundamentals of our Faith: the divinity of Christ, the resurrection from the dead of His true Body, our own immortality, and so forth.

On February 6th of this year, Pope John Paul II addressed a group of priests gathered in Rome to study parish missions. The Pope admonished them that, before beginning their deliberations, they should look around them and see what has been happening to the faithful. The Pope said that what they see will force them "to admit that the *majority* of Christians today feel bewildered, confused, perplexed and even misled by widely disseminated ideas that contradict revealed truth." He told priests that "it is necessary today to be patient, and *to begin all over again from the very beginning of faith.*"[2]

These are strong words and of enormous significance to today's catechist. You cannot be too clear in the presentation of the doctrine of the Faith. Note carefully that the Pope implies that Christians are being confused not by what is happening outside the Church—one is always on guard against admitted enemies—but against what is being said in some quarters within the Church. It seems to me that the confusion to which the Holy Father referred stems in great part precisely from taking a one-sided view of Jesus to suit preconceived models about what He should have said and should have done. For example, some pick the virtue of social justice and attempt to exhaust all Christian doctrine in its application, effectively distorting both the virtue itself and the doctrine of the Savior. The result of such eclectic glimpses of Jesus is to set in false opposition life experience and catechetical content, method and spontaneity, morality and freedom, memory and understanding. Such antitheses are artificial and will not arise if the *whole* Jesus is presented to the faithful, but they will, of course, inevitably appear if Jesus is shown as merely the perfect man rather than the Divine Son of Mary, the Word made flesh.

Jesus Christ is the Word without whom was made nothing that was made. Who has spoken this Word? The Father: "The word you hear is not mine; it comes from the Father who sent me" (Jn. 14:24). We can know the Father, then, only through the Son (Jn. 6:46), and it is this Son of God whom the catechist must announce to his or her catechumens if they are to attain a knowledge and ever deeper love of God Himself. But the goal of the catechist is not to train his charges to parrot doctrinal texts, for "none of those who cry 'Lord, Lord,' will enter the kingdom of heaven, but only the one who does the will of my Father in heaven" (Mt. 7:19). The catechist's aim, therefore, is to turn out disciples of the Lord in response to our Lord's parting instruction to "make disciples of all nations" (Mt. 28:19), that is, followers of the Lord who are not content to know what He said but "to put on the Lord Jesus Christ" (Rom. 13:14).

It seems to me, then, that, if we truly grasp what the Holy Father has intended to do by using the Christological approach in *Catechesi tradendae*, namely to present a balanced, integral Christian message, we shall immediately be able to identify and avoid most of the present day catechetical excesses, which generally result from minimizing or even excluding from catechesis those qualities of our Lord seen to be incompatible with novelties favored by this or that fashionable theological school. We must receive Jesus and preach Jesus exactly as the Father sent Him to us, and doctrinal fads which distort the real Jesus must be avoided like the proverbial plague.

The Faithful Are Hungry for the Truth

It would be clearly a mistake to suppose that Supreme Pontiffs make poor catechists, because their heavy administrative burdens and the isolation in which they are popularly supposed to live prevents them from contact with the realities of the world of men. Anyone who has seen Pope John Paul II in action in St. Peter's Square week after week, and in Roman parishes Sunday after Sunday, not to mention his pastoral excursions around the world, can testify with total candor that the Holy Father is a born catechist. He establishes immediate rapport with the crowds and especially with the young, who have flocked around him in Galway, Tokyo and Madison Square Garden with palpable joy. People who have heard him speak frequently report: "The Pope was talking right to me." The crowds applaud him everywhere even when he makes, as he seldom fails to do, spiritual demands of them. This phenomenon of an exacting teacher with the attractiveness of a popular hero has puzzled not a few observers within and outside the Church.

A recent newspaper poll in Europe found that John Paul II was considered the most admired personality in a certain country which had just approved abortion by a two to one margin. The memory of his triumphal visit to the United States is, I am sure, still fresh in your minds, but many have wondered why he was so well received when he was so blunt about divorce; an all-male, celibate priesthood; and the role of the Church in politics. The Pope's visit was equally cheered in Latin America, also, even though he had some sobering observations to make about the so-called liberation theology. How can we explain the spontaneous acceptance of a leader who condemns the conduct of the very people he is addressing?

The first explanation may be that the abuses the Pope condemns are indulged in by fewer people than we are led to believe. But the best explanation, it seems to me, lies in the simple fact that men and women everywhere are hungry for the truth, and that God gives them the grace to recognize the truth when it is offered to them. Are not the faithful themselves "a letter from Christ written...not on tablets of stone, but on tablets of human hearts"? (2 Cor. 3:3) Every man and woman knows deep in his and her heart the difference between right and wrong and instinctively respects the teacher who faithfully and fearlessly declares it; and their spirit is willing, though their flesh may be weak. We all welcome the voice that calls us to rise above our own weaknesses.

No doubt the Pope has great personal charm, but his impact on the faithful, and even on those who are not fully united with the Church, is surely due principally to his courage in teaching the Faith of his fathers. He is kind; he is patient; he is forgiving; and one gets the impression that it would pain him personally to hurt anyone. But when he has finished speaking, the audience knows that he expects sacrifice of them, for deep down they recognize with him that "the gate is narrow and the way is hard that leads to life" (Mt. 7:13).

The Priest and Catechesis

The Pope fills his role of catechist to the world with great naturalness probably because he was brought up in a strong catechetical tradition in Poland, where to this day the priest is the central figure in the catechetical apostolate. The pastor may seek the help of assistants, as he is obliged to do in the larger parishes, and his helpers may be other priests or unordained ministers, both lay and religious, but the chief catechist in every Polish parish is the priest, which I would favor everywhere, just as the bishop is the first teacher of the Faith in every diocese and the Pope the first teacher of the Faith in the universal Church.

I emphasize the role of priests in catechetics, not, certainly, to diminish the role of religious and laity, particularly of women—without women the world's catechesis would virtually collapse overnight—but to urge priests to recognize their responsibility and to fulfill it in this regard. The Vatican Council II directives include a reminder to priests that "they should lead all the faithful by means of catechetical instruction...to a full knowledge of the mystery of salvation,"[3] and that probably explains why the office of the Holy See charged with responsibility for catechesis in the universal Church is located in the Congregation for the Clergy, for Vatican II also declares that the Word of God "is quite rightly sought from the mouth of priests."[4]

The role of Pope, bishop and priest in catechetics is obviously multiple, for the catechesis of millions of people involves more than direct teaching. It involves organization, preparation of teachers, selection of texts, good example, inspiration and all the other ingredients of a vast educational program. The point is that superiors must keep a finger on all this activity. Middle management is necessary, but the fact that it is gradated does not signify that it ceases to be middle, *for the teaching authority still depends on the hierarchical Church, as we will see in more detail later on. It is not demeaning to obey rather than to legislate, for, after all, we are all members of the one Body of Christ*, and each has his or her specific role and ought to perform it with humility and love (Rom. 12:3ff.).

There is no need to summarize for you here the contents of *Catechesi tradendae;* you have all read it, I hope, several times. But I should like to highlight a few points which seem to be of particular significance to the American scene. The points I shall touch are five: 1) pluralism and the truth; 2) catechesis of old and young; 3) the catechist is one sent; 4) revelation and the signs of the times; 5) the catechist and the Kingdom.

Pluralism and the Truth

"Cuius regio et eius religio" is a dictum that no longer corresponds to reality in the Western world. I shall not attempt to trace its evolution from the times when no other religion was tolerated in a given country than that of its ruler, to our times in which, to a greater or lesser extent, adherents of diverse religious persuasions live

together in relative peace. Religious pluralism is a fact of our modern world, a sign of the times if you will, and there is perhaps no more pluralistic society in the entire world than the United States, as I do not have to point out to you.

Freedom publicly to profess one's belief is, of course, a blessing for us Catholics, for it allows us full observance of the liturgy of our Faith and the opportunity to be schooled in our Faith and to pass it on to our children. But, on the other hand, it does expose us to other people whose beliefs and practices may threaten what we hold most dear and which may tempt us to abandon truth and fall into error. There is no way in this world of ours to isolate ourselves effectively from the bad example of others or sometimes even to avoid confrontation on important issues concerning which we may hold positions radically opposed to those of fellow citizens.

Catechists must face, then, the enormous challenge of forming Catholics of all ages to live safely and faithfully in this pluralistic society. What must they do to meet this challenge successfully? Catechists must learn, first of all, to identify those values in people not of our Faith which Catholics can accept and even cordially share, because they respond to the nature of man, and to distinguish them from those values which contradict the nature of man. Catholics are proud to work with men and women of every religious persuasion who defend the dignity of man, but, even in the name of peace, Catholics are not free to espouse theories and practices which violate the God-given nature which man has received.

When it comes to dealing with people who profess religions similar to our own, catechists should be taught to recognize that many of our separated brothers and sisters believe at least some of the essential doctrines of our Faith, but catechists must train their students to recognize teachings of other Christian religions which do not fully conform in essentials with Catholic doctrine, and which Catholics must therefore reject, even when doing so will delay that union and cooperation which good men everywhere so ardently desire. If differing tenets and practices in other religions flow mainly from cultural and linguistic variations, there may be some room for ecumenical maneuver, but when it is a question of essential doctrine it would not be honest for either side to make superficial concessions to express a fundamental unity which, in fact, would not exist.

Catechists should teach their charges to respect legitimate pluralism and to promote the sound ecumenical activity which the Church of our times has rightly called for, but catechists must inculcate this respect without "neglecting to teach that the fullness of revealed truths and the means of salvation instituted by Christ are found in the Catholic Church."[5]

Pope John Paul I, while Archbishop of Venice, wrote a book entitled *Illustrissimi*. In it he recounts Tolstoy's fable about the king, the blind men and the elephants. One day the king herded the royal elephants together and gathered the blind of the kingdom around them. The king then told the blind people to reach out and touch the animals and describe to him what elephants were like. One blind man touched a tail and said that elephants were like poles with brushes on the end. Another felt a leg and said that elephants were like walking columns. A third touched a trunk and said that elephants were like thick ropes.[6]

Papa Luciani's point, of course, was that careless pluralism results in a distorted view of things. No detail gives the whole picture and is, in fact, false, unless somehow it can be made to fit logically into the whole. Therefore, the principle of pluralism cannot be used to justify the validity of contradictory ideas. So, while catechists must be trained to teach their charges to respect the intellectual freedom of those not of our Faith and to respect also their good will, catechists must beware of extending the limits of pluralism to the point that details are allowed to obscure the whole. Legitimate pluralism is an aspect of religious freedom and means that "all men should be immune from coercion...so that, within due limits, nobody is forced to act against his convictions in religious matters."[7] It does not mean that man is morally free to decide on what is right and wrong for him regardless of the precepts of the divine and natural law.

Catechesis of Old and Young

The second point I wish to discuss is perhaps more implicit in *Catechesi tradendae* than explicit. Pope John Paul II reminds us that "the specific purpose of catechesis...is to develop, with God's help, a still germinal faith, and also to advance in fullness and to nourish day by day the Christian life of the faithful, both *old* and *young*."[8]

One might think it unrealistic, and even a bit patronizing, to call for teaching formal classes of religion to older people. After all, most of them are already raising families of their own, or have raised them, have been teaching the Faith to their own children and have probably given good religious advice to friends and neighbors over the years. What need, then, is there to make a special point of catechizing adults? One mother of ten children recently complained, for example, that she was tired of having to run up to the parish hall for another course on Baptism every time she had another child. "I know more about Baptism now than the priest," she exclaimed.

Overly zealous pastors apart, there is little doubt that today's Catholics have need to study their Faith and deepen their knowledge of the Scriptures over a much longer period of time than did their forebears. The half-life of medicine is said to be five years. This means that a young man who graduates from medical school today will discover that half of what he learned will no longer be valid in 1986. While the core of the Faith remains the same and always will, sometimes it seems to me that the half-life of some of the ecclesiastical sciences cannot be much more than five years either. For example, scarcely have we begun to unravel the moral implications of nuclear energy, when we are confronted by the terrifying implications of genetic manipulation. Scripture scholars have only, perhaps, scratched the surface of the full meaning of the Dead Sea Scrolls in the study of the Bible, before a library of clay tablets dug up elsewhere presents new problems of biblical interpretation. Modern archaeology has forced all of us back to the books, and certainly Vatican Council II dramatically stimulated religious research within and outside the Church all over the world.

Religious formation cannot, then, be considered over when a child makes his or her Confirmation. We priests have become aware ever since the Council how necessary it is to continue our reading and even to do formal study once in a while, so as to be able merely to keep up. Today's laity continues its education far beyond primary school, and so its religious education and formation needs must continue far beyond what might have been sufficient preparation in decades past. As we approach the twenty-first century, the image of catechists, then, must include that of people capable of forming adult Catholics to cope with the ever-changing world in which they live. Thus we have the need for catechetical institutes like St. John's Institute for Advanced Studies in Christian Doctrine, to supplement institutes preparing the traditional and much needed grass-roots catechists on the parish and neighborhood level.

My emphasis on adult catechesis must not, of course, cause us to forget that the title and purpose of the Catechetical Synod of 1977 concerned young people in particular,[9] for it is evident that the young remain the primary object of the Church's catechetical solicitude. Universities are useless unless supplied with students who were taught to read and write in elementary schools. So, too, are advanced courses in theology, unless aspirants to these have first been taught their prayers and the essentials of their religion.

The Catechist Is One Sent

The third point revolves around the notion of mission. A catechist is a man or woman sent by the Church as Christ was sent by His Father. "I came, not of my own accord, but he sent me" (Jn. 8:42). And again: "As the Father has sent me, even so I send you" (Jn. 20:21). Forty-two times, if my count is right, St. John speaks of Jesus as having been *sent* by the Father. So, to adapt the Letter to the Hebrews, the catechist "does not take this honor on his own initiative, but only when called by God" (Heb. 5:4).

This is an extremely important concept because, unless the catechist is sent directly or indirectly by the Church, he or she is not authorized to teach the Faith of the Church. While it is true that "he who is not against us is for us" (Mk. 9:40), catechumens have no guarantee that the doctrine they are receiving is reliable, unless their catechist is truly sent by the Church—parents are missioned by the very fact that they are parents, it goes without saying.

The corollary of this is that the catechist is obliged to teach what the Church believes rather than what might be his or her personal opinion. "Every catechist must constantly endeavor to transmit, by his teaching and behavior, the teaching and life of Christ. He will not seek to keep directed toward himself, and toward his personal opinions and attitudes, the attention and consent of the mind and heart of the person he is catechizing. Above all, he will not try to inculcate his personal opinions and options, as if these were expressed by Christ's teachings and by the lessons of His life."[10] On the contrary, the catechist must say with our Lord: "My teaching is not mine, but his who sent me" (Jn. 7:16). It would be anomalous, indeed, if a catechist of whatever level would pretend to a doctrinal autonomy that the Messiah Himself did not profess.

The voice of the catechist, then, must echo the voice of the Church. Jesus Christ is the message that must be found on the catechist's tongue, and if it is, the catechist will feel peace within himself or herself. But faithful transmission of the Word will not render the catechist immune from the attacks of others, for the fate of the disciple will not differ from that of the Master (Jn. 16:20). Though Jesus was God, not everyone accepted what He taught, as we well know. Sometimes men rejected what He said, not from bad will, but just because they were too dull to understand, and in this case our Lord patiently explained (Mt. 13:36ff.), but at other times men rejected him because of the hardness of their hearts, even in His Apostles (Mk. 16:14), or for the apparent want of divine grace at a given moment (Jn. 6:63ff.). But, regardless of the reason why men rejected Him, Jesus did not change His teachings to make them more palatable. He did not come to seek popularity or consensus and was not prepared to buy friends at the price of truth. On one occasion, the announcement of the Eucharist, He was saddened when so many walked out on Him, but was prepared to lose all His followers rather than withdraw His teaching, and we can almost feel the trepidation in the heart of Christ when He asked His Apostles: "Will you also go away?" (Jn. 6:67)

The catechist, therefore, must realize that the success he or she is seen to achieve, as demonstrated by the visible deepening of faith in the catechumens, will depend much more on invisible factors than on pedagogical skill and the mastery of psychology. I do not make this point to belittle the necessary technical training catechists should have, nor their obligation to learn how to command the attention and form the attitudes of their charges. Jesus Himself worked miracles to attract attention, and used parables to influence His hearers with emotional examples, and He did not fail to instruct us to use our talents to the full (Mt. 25:14). I make the point merely to warn catechists against the temptation to dilute Christian doctrine to make it more attractive to some of its critics.

If a catechist teaches the Faith in the spirit and with the integrity with which it was handed on to him or to her, then there is no reason to be discouraged, regardless of visible results. The catechist's technical skills are not to be disregarded in the total formation process, and you and I have spent enough years in school to know that some teachers are better than others, but we also know that the skill of the teacher is of secondary importance in religious formation. For the student looks to the teacher first for example, and that is why those who are known to have abandoned serious religious obligations, which they once freely assumed, are not to be preferred as catechists.

But the student himself, of course, plays a vital part in the learning process and the catechist must realize that the soil of the student's heart is not always prepared to receive the seed of the Word of God, as Jesus so graphically revealed in the parable of the sower (Mt. 13:18). These are the times when both catechist and catechumen must resort in special fervor to prayer and fasting (Mt. 17:20). But youth is especially generous and willing to sacrifice life itself for an ideal about which it is convinced. So, while our Lord must be presented as He describes Himself, "meek and humble of heart," He must also be presented as one who has come "to spread not peace, but division" (Mt. 10:34), for youth can identify with a strong Christ, if the purpose of strength is made clear. If by teaching the truth the catechist is accused of being divisive, he must realize that this is not a sin, for this is why Jesus came.

Revelation and the Signs of the Times

The fourth point I wish to discuss is the relationship that exists between revelation and the signs of the times. *Catechesi tradendae* tackles the question head on: "The first question of a general kind that presents itself here concerns the danger and the temptation to mix catechetical teaching unduly with overt or masked ideological views.... It is on the basis of revelation that catechesis will try to set its course, revelation as transmitted by the universal Magisterium of the Church, in its solemn or ordinary form."[11] We know that divine public revelation ceased with the death of St. John the Evangelist. There have been many people who through the centuries have claimed to have received private revelations from heaven, but the Church does not propose for public belief even the most convincing of these.

On the other hand, Vatican Council II called on us to search the signs of the times for authentic indications of the presence of God and of His plans in a given moment and in given circumstances: "The people of God believes that it is led by the Spirit of the Lord who fills the whole world. Moved by that faith, it tries to discern in the events, the needs and the longings which it shares with other men of our time, what may be the genuine signs of the presence or of the purpose of God."[12] Can this mean that, instead of having ceased with St. John, public divine revelation continues even today and can be read in the signs of the times of each passing generation?

In the Catholic sense, revelation is not revelation unless it certainly comes from God. Since the above Conciliar text speaks of signs that *"may* be genuine" we cannot consider them to be revelation in the strict sense. I think that most of us realize this, because almost everyone has his or her own opinion about the significance of this or that "sign of the times." How do we know, then, what the signs of the times are demanding of us? We cannot know from their intrinsic meaning, but only from confronting them with the Word of God as transmitted by the Church.

When the Council called on the Bark of Peter to scrutinize the signs of the times, it wished to remind the Church that she was not a blind ship racing through the seas of time heedless of winds, waves and shoals and deaf to the cries of the shipwrecked pleading to be saved. No, the Church is a living ship, with lookouts posted to warn of storm and iceberg, and pilot alert to every change of current, ready to take on board the storm-tossed longing for salvation.

The signs of the times are not infallible keys to the divine mind, but opportunities and warnings along the Church's route to heaven which must be interpreted within the context of the revelation we have already received. The only proven chart of the sea of life remains the Word of God as transmitted to us by the Church, for without the Church we would be on a very uncertain journey, indeed.

The Kingdom of God

My fifth and last point concerns the kingdom of God, the catechist's conception of which must, of course, be made that of the Church. The problem lies in the degree to which temporal progress can be equated with the growth of the kingdom of God. The kingdom of God is not the kingdom of Caesar. Caesar has his rights, which must be respected (Mt. 22:21; 1 Pt. 2:13ff.), but so does God have His claim on us, it goes without saying. As a matter of fact we are told to "seek *first* the kingdom of God" (Mt. 6:33), and this in preference to food, drink and life itself.

Vatican Council II points out that "although we must be careful to distinguish earthly progress clearly from the increase of the kingdom of God, such progress is of vital concern to the kingdom of God, insofar as it can contribute to the better ordering of the kingdom of God."[13] That is to say, earthly progress is not an end in itself, but is useful when it strengthens the kingdom of God among men. This becomes clearer when we note that the same Council points to the saints[14] and to religious[15] as special signs of the existence of the kingdom of God, that is, of a kingdom that is not of this world, as our Lord Himself clearly revealed (Jn. 18:36).

The fact is that the catechist has no special competence *qua* catechist to discuss and to teach the means to be used to bring about temporal progress, and when the catechist steps into the field of finance, or politics, or sociology, and so forth, he or she is stepping out of his or her role of a catechist sent by the Church. The catechist, therefore, exceeds his or her mandate, if he or she gives the impression that his or her mission from the Church is to teach other than Jesus Christ and Him crucified (cf. 1 Cor. 1:23), or that this mission includes committing the Church to this or that political or other purely secular option. The Church claims no expertise in the secular sciences because she has no expertise in them as Church, and it is wrong for anyone to pretend that she does.

Now, when the catechist, in imitation of Christ, "goes to preach the good news of the kingdom of God to the other cities also" (Lk. 4:43), he should have in mind "to preach the Gospel to the whole of creation" (Mk. 16:15), so he does not hesitate to go into "the highways and hedges and to compel people to come in" (Lk. 14:23), by the force of his example and conviction of his teaching, not, of course, by coercion, moral or otherwise. The point is that the catechist's purpose in going "to the other cities" is not to *find* something there, but to bring Someone there. He does not go to discover the kingdom of God already present, but to announce and to bring it. It is important to ponder this thought, because there has been a certain tendency here and there to dilute Christian teaching to try to make it conform to behavior which is objectively at odds with Christian morality, and to take it for granted that the kingdom of God already exists everywhere even among those who have not yet been "born again of water and the Spirit" (Jn. 3:5). This would not make God's kingdom come, but would only serve to divide it, and a divided kingdom cannot stand (cf. Mk. 3:24).

When the Holy Father went to Japan earlier this year, he asked a group of religious leaders of the Orient what the Catholic Church could presume to bring to people already so richly endowed with beautiful traditions, a rich culture and material well-being. Answering his own question, the Pope declared: "It is Jesus Christ we proclaim. We bring His name and His message of joy to all peoples, and while we sincerely respect their cultures and traditions, we respectfully invite them to listen to Him and open their hearts to Him."[16] Like the Holy Father, the catechist, also, must preach Jesus Christ as Lord (cf. 2 Cor. 4:5), respectfully, yes, but clearly and courageously.

Conclusion

The field of catechesis is a vast one, and you will be the first to agree that it is not exhausted by the Apostolic Exhortation *Catechesi tradendae*, even when this is read, as it should be, in conjunction with *Evangelii nuntiandi* of Pope Paul VI.[17] There remain, consequently, many points which I should have liked to discuss with you; for example, the utility of a universal outline of Catholic doctrine to guide authors and publishers in producing reliable national, regional and local catechisms[18]; the correct sequence for the reception of the Sacraments of Initiation, which has deviated in some places along emotional instead of theological directions[19]; the importance of memory in religious formation, which is no less than it is in other disciplines.[20]

But these topics and many others that you might be thinking of can be explored with confidence under the guidance of your local Bishops who have already labored so fruitfully for the publication of your National Catechetical Directory, and who have had the foresight to establish Catechetical Institutes in so many of their dioceses to form faithful and competent catechists all over the United States.

There is nothing magical about the year 2000, but as we approach such a milestone in the history of man and particularly in the history of salvation, there is a great temptation to prophesy what will take place in the third millennium. As we mentioned earlier, human knowledge is passing through an age of explosion. Structures both civil and ecclesiastical are evolving, and the Church must make the necessary adjustments. But permit me to caution you against those who foresee that future catechesis will be all in this direction or all in that direction; that family catechesis will replace Sunday school, that the CCD will replace the parish school, and so forth. There surely will be changes to be made, but you Americans have a very wise saying about putting all the eggs in one basket. Meeting new challenges does not necessarily involve discarding all the successful operations of the past and starting from the beginning as if experience had taught nothing. There is no method or approach that will respond to every situation, so while new approaches may be added, for example, more emphasis on family catechesis, there is certainly no reason to close down other methods which are, in fact, producing good fruit. Parochial school, pastors, CCD, religion coordinators, family catechesis, diocesan director, lay men and women catechists, religious catechists, the Bishop himself, all have their necessary places in the catechetical apostolate of today and of tomorrow.

The Catholic Church in the United States is entering upon her third century of organized existence and finds itself in a splendid position to expand under God. But God needs catechists, men and women so imbued with the Word themselves, that they are restless until they communicate it. I wish to take this opportunity to praise and thank from the bottom of my heart all those who are dedicating their time and strength so enthusiastically, often at great sacrifice, to the work of catechesis, and, in a particular way, those engaged in the formation of catechists. This Symposium, which will surely produce abundant spiritual fruit, is visible testimony to the effectiveness of Catechetical Institutes, and its success will give comfort and renewed strength not only to those catechists who have personally participated, but also to those who will feel the impact of it. My special thanks goes to Msgr. George A. Kelly, Director of the Catechetical Institute at St. John's and to his collaborators who have planned the Symposium. It is a great privilege to be the catechetical partner of such dedicated people in our glorious burden of spreading the fruit.

Finally, I pray with you that you will continue to use responsibly your precious freedom, not only to deepen the faith in those already within the fold, but also to share the faith with the multitude of the unchurched in your country who are ripe for the harvest, for, consciously or not, every man and woman is waiting to be gathered into one fold under one Shepherd. After all, your freedom would be a selfish boast, if you did not use it to respond to the unspoken plea of your brothers and sisters in your midst, who are yearning to hear the Good News, the message from Jesus Christ.

FOOTNOTES

1. Pope John Paul II. Apostolic Exhortation *Catechesi tradendae*. Oct. 16, 1979 *(AAS* vol. 71, pp. 1277-1340), no. 60.
2. Pope John Paul II. *L'Osservatore Romano*, Feb. 7, 1981, no. 31, p. 1.
3. Vatican Council II. *Christus Dominus*, no. 30.
4. Vatican Council II. *Presbyterorum ordinis*, no. 48.
5. *Catechesi tradendae*, no. 32.
6. Luciani, Albino. *Illustrissimi*. Little, Brown & Co., Boston, 1978, pp. 215-216.
7. Vatican Council II. *Dignitatis humanae*, no. 2.
8. *Catechesi tradendae*, no. 7.
9. Synod of Bishops, 1977. "Message to the People of God." *L'Osservatore Romano*, Oct. 30, 1977, p. 1.
10. *Catechesi tradendae*, no. 5.
11. *Ibid.*, no. 52.
12. Vatican Council II. *Gaudium et spes*, no. 11.
13. *Ibid.*, no. 39.
14. Vatican Council II. *Lumen gentium*, no. 50.
15. *Ibid.*, no. 44.
16. Pope John Paul II. *L'Osservatore Romano*, Supplemento "Giovanni Paolo in Medio Oriente," Feb. 24, 1981, no. 40, p. 63.
17. **Pope Paul VI. Apostolic Exhortation *Evangelii nuntiandi*. Dec. 8, 1975**, *(AAS* vol. 68, 1976, pp. 5-76).
18. *Catechesi tradendae*, no. 50.
19. Sacred Congregation for the Clergy. *General Catechetical Directory*. London, 1972, pp. 100ff.
20. *Catechesi tradendae*, no. 55.

CHAPTER ONE

A Pastoral View of Catechetics

Most Rev. Anthony J. Bevilacqua, J.C.D., J.D.
Auxiliary Bishop-Chancellor
of the Diocese of Brooklyn

Introduction

The Apostolic Exhortation, *Catechesi tradendae*, characterizes catechesis as a pastoral activity. It is a pastoral ministry whose specific aim is "to develop with God's help an as yet initial faith, and to advance in fullness and to nourish day by day the Christian life of the faithful, young and old."[1]

Catechesis is to be distinguished from those forms of religious education which have as their main but important task instruction as an academic enterprise. Catechesis utilizes instruction but its specific goal is to make a person's faith become "living, conscious and active through the light of instruction and to lead communities and individuals to maturity of faith."[2]

As a pastoral ministry, catechesis is an activity by the whole Church, to the whole Church, for the whole Church. It utilizes all the resources of the Church—scripture, theology, liturgy, law, history, life experiences and Christian witness. It applies the data of these resources in a living transmission of the Word of God but always in accordance with the Magisterium of the Church.

Catechesis is a pastoral activity by all the faithful of the Church: the Pope, Bishops, clergy, religious and laity. Catechesis is a pastoral ministry to and with all the faithful of the Church: faithful of all ages, of all conditions, of all states of life, of all economic levels, of all cultures, languages and races.

In the fulfillment of its pastoral function, catechesis brings God to the individual and the community, and the individual and community to God. It utilizes that which is usefully appropriate from the human sciences about man: anthropology, sociology, psychology, pedagogy, etc.

The unity of the Church's pastoral mission—the salvation of souls—integrates catechesis with all other pastoral activities of the Church and, in particular, with the liturgical life of the Church, the ministry of service and the emerging ministry of communication. But as a pastoral ministry among many pastoral activities, catechesis must hold a chief priority.

The task of this presentation is not to describe the principles and general programs of catechesis. This has been admirably elucidated on the universal level in *Catechesi tradendae* as well as in two other papal documents: the *General Catechetical Directory* and the Apostolic Exhortation of Pope Paul VI, *On Evangelization in the Modern World*. On the national level of United States catechetics, this was equally well done in several works issued by the American hierarchy: the Pastoral Letter, *To Teach as Jesus Did* (1972), the document, *Basic Teachings for Catholic Religious Education* (1973), and the *National Catechetical Directory* entitled *Sharing the Light of Faith* (1977).

My function is rather to attempt a description of the present state of the pastoral ministry of catechesis in our nation and to focus on one segment of the nation, the Diocese of Brooklyn.

By surveying the status of catechesis on the national level and the level of the Diocese of Brooklyn, it can be stated at the very outset that, for the most part, each scene reflects the other. The Diocese of Brooklyn is a microcosm of the nation and the nation is a macrocosm of the diocese. There is generally a reinforcement and corroboration of the program evaluations, problems, achievements, principles, priorities and recommendations affecting catechesis in both target areas.

Much of the data used for this presentation is taken from several survey reports issued between 1976-1981 on the national and diocesan level. One of the diocesan studies consists of a survey on catechesis that I made in the Spring of 1981 throughout the diocese. A questionnaire was sent to the 221 parishes of the diocese with responses from 107.

The paper can be divided into four major sections:

I. What is the present state of catechetical impact or Catholicity in our nation and in the Diocese of Brooklyn?

II. What are the problems of catechesis on the national and Brooklyn diocesan level?

III. What are the positive achievements of catechesis on the national and Brooklyn diocesan level?

IV. In the light of the present state of the pastoral ministry of catechesis in the nation and in the Diocese of Brooklyn, what are the major pastoral observations, priorities and recommendations that can affect catechesis?

I. Present State of Catechetical Impact or Catholicity in the Nation and in the Diocese of Brooklyn

A. NATION

1. 1976-1978 Studies on Catholicity of American Children and Youth

In the years 1976 to 1978, there appeared a series of four studies on the religious knowledge, attitudes and practices of Catholic children and youth in the United States. These studies revealed a growing number of children and young not receiving any formal Catholic education as well as an increased rejection of the Church as a teacher by our young Catholics. A summary of the statistics and conclusions of these four studies painted the following picture of our Catholic children and youth in the period covered by the studies.[3]

1. Between 1965 and 1975, the number of elementary school age Catholics not receiving any religious education whatsoever rose from 1,677,752 to 3,272,757. This represents an increase of nearly 100%.

2. Those receiving religious instruction dropped from 7,978,855 to 4,469,313. This represents on the elementary school level a decrease of 1.5 million.

3. The proportion of children on the elementary school level receiving no formal religious education nearly doubled from 17.3% to 33.59%.

4. On the high school age level, the number of Catholic youth not receiving any religious instruction whatsoever rose from 1,412,346 to 3,409,222. This represents an increase of slightly less than 2,000,000.

5. The proportion of high school students not participating in any formal religious instruction rose from 36.47% to 64.10%.

6. The total number of elementary and secondary school students receiving no formal instruction whatsoever grew from 3,090,098 in 1965 to 6,681,980 in 1975.

7. The proportion of elementary and high school students receiving no formal instruction whatsoever went from 22.85% in 1965 to 44.37% in 1975. This represents an increase of almost 100%.

8. While past research has documented the beginning of religious doubt about the age of 17 or 18, the latest research reports that the age of first religious doubts has dropped an average of two years since 1948 so that there are even the beginning of religious doubts at the age of 13.

9. There is no projection of an immediate rise in religious practice or traditional orthodoxy among Catholics. Religion is not central in the lives of most people but is more a recourse to be tapped in need. The young may remain identified with the Church but in a less formal and traditional fashion.

10. Weekly church attendance will not be considered an imperative, and a plurality of beliefs will exist.

11. Children in Catholic elementary school are ignorant of many religious code words. They are also fuzzy about the meaning and purpose of the Church, especially as an institution. They have a poor knowledge of scriptures. They are also confused about many of the major doctrines of the Church such as teaching on the Blessed Mother, grace, resurrection, faith as a gift, purpose of marriage. But at the same time, it must be stated that in over 50% of questions asked them in a survey on religious knowledge they did quite well.

In 1976, 8.6 million children and young persons enrolled in formal religious education programs. The statistics given above, showing that 6,681,980 elementary and high school students were not receiving any religious instruction whatsoever led to the famous question: "Where are the 6.6 million?" The figures can be frightening. Where the 6.6 million are presents a pastoral challenge as well as an educational one. Its solution will demand additional information and research in addition to prudent decisions and concrete, effective programs of pastoral action.

Since those studies in 1976-1978, there have been more recent studies on the religious knowledge, attitude and practices of our children, youth and young adults. These more recent studies continue the trend of the early studies by revealing a growing number of our Catholic children and youth not receiving any formal Catholic education as well as an increased rejection of the Church as a teacher, particularly by the young and young adults.

2. National Opinion Research Center Report/ Knights of Columbus Research Study—1981

Recently the National Opinion Research Center completed a study on "Catholic Schools and Catholic Youth, Commitment and Community." The study was sponsored by the Knights of Columbus and was presented to the 78th Annual Convention of the National Catholic Education Association in New York City held April 20-23, 1981. The study was presented by Dr. William C. McCready of the University of Chicago.

As with most studies of this nature, it had good news and bad news.

The survey polled 2,170 randomly selected Catholics between the ages of 14-29.

Its general conclusions regarding Catholic Schools and their impact on youth were rather positive:

1. That Catholic Schools are an important element in what is termed a religious "turning point" which occurs for many in the late 20's.

2. That Catholic Schools are increasing their influence on the lives of people who attend them, independent of family background.

Professor McCready suggests that the reason for the positive influence of Catholic Schools is that they connect the individual into the local Catholic community more closely.

The study also provides information on the amount of religious instruction received by young adults. Of those between the ages of 18 to 30, 13% have received no religious education or instruction whatsoever. Of those who attended public high school, 73% stated that there were years when they did not receive any religious instruction whatsoever. The reasons for no religious instruction received by the 73% had little to do, according to Dr. McCready, with the quality of religious instruction offered. Thus 50% stated that the reason was lack of interest in religion. 36% gave as their reason either that their friends were not going to religious instruction, or that their parents did not care, or that they already knew enough about religion.

In this area of the amount of religious instruction received, we can summarize the conclusion by stating:

1. During elementary school years, there is a greater percentage receiving religious education at some time in this period.

2. In high school, according to Professor McCready, the number receiving some form of religious instruction drops dramatically for reasons that have much more to do with peer pressure and religious indifference on the part of parents and children than they do with the Church's efforts to organize religious instruction.

The study showed that Catholic Schools have a significant beneficial impact on the young and young adults:

1. Catholic Schools seem to be a very important part of the rebound effect that occurs in the late 20's. According to Professor McCready, this is an important part of future stability and religious well-being of Catholic families.

2. There is a significant difference between those with eight years of Catholic education and those with less in the areas of Mass attendance, reception of the Eucharist, belief in life after death, whether or not one has thought of a vocation, whether or not one reads Catholic periodicals, whether or not one has participated in a study group, whether or not one is opposed to abortion.

3. The beneficial impact of Catholic Schools today is much more important than it has been in the past when

society was basically more friendly towards the values that our tradition represents.

The report indicates several reasons for the beneficial impact of Catholic Schools:

1. That Catholic Schools promote greater closeness in connection with the local community. This closeness in connection with the community endures into adulthood.

2. For most Catholics, "Church" is the local parish Church. The parish provides a context for the process by which individual families acquire values and pass them along.

3. Almost half the difference on the Catholicity scale is accounted for simply by the fact that those who have gone to Catholic Schools feel that they are closer to the Church. Dr. McCready reports that the difference is independent of family background and influence of the spouse. He says it can be considered to be "pure Catholic School effect." The result of attendance in Catholic School is that Catholic Schools integrate young people more closely into the Catholic community through the institutional affiliation.

In the area of religious practice, belief in certain doctrines of the Church and acceptance of the Church's teaching on moral values, the news from the report is not so good:

1. Thus 37% attend Mass weekly. 25% attend Mass only once a year. 38% therefore do not attend Mass at all. In other words, 63% attend Mass either once a year or not at all.

2. On doctrinal issues, 64% believe in life after death. Only 44% believe it is a sin to miss Mass. 75% do not believe in the infallibility of the Pope on faith or morals.

3. In the area of moral issues, there is less adherence to the Church's position.

    a. On birth control, in the ages of 18 to 29, only 5% agree with the Church's position.

b. On the question of remarriage for the divorced, only 11% agree with the Church's position.

c. Regarding the wrongfulness of pre-marital sex, only 17% agree with the Church's teaching.

d. The only two issues on which the majority of young adults agree with the Church's position are homosexuality and abortion on demand.

It would seem that one can conclude that religious instruction, whether given in Catholic Schools or outside of Catholic Schools, has no effect on belief and acceptance of certain teachings of the Church, whether they think living together before marriage is sinful, whether or not they think birth control is wrong, whether or not it is sinful to remarry unlawfully after divorce.

B. DIOCESE OF BROOKLYN

1. 1980—R.E.O.I.— Religious Knowledge Survey of Catholic Elementary Schools in the Diocese of Brooklyn

Where our Catholic students are at in the knowledge of their Catholic religion and in their religious attitude is indicated in a 1980 study conducted in the Diocese of Brooklyn. The study used the Religious Education Outcomes Inventory (R.E.O.I.). The survey covered 4,158 Eighth Grade Catholic School children in 77 Catholic Schools in the diocese and compared the results to the National Scale.

The diocesan average for the first section on religious knowledge, for all practical purposes, matches the national average. The following table compared the national average to the 1980 Brooklyn Diocese average in the six major categories.

	National Schools	Diocese of Brooklyn Schools	National Parish C.C.D.
God	63.4	63.6	56.4
Church	55.2	54.7	46.3
Sacraments	77.03	77.8	69.9
Church Life	66.9	65.4	60.7
Scripture	60.4	59.1	50.7
Religious Terms	59.3	58.9	50.9

CHURCH

The weakest area lies in the students' understanding of Church: its meaning, its structure in functioning, Ecumenism and the knowledge of Mary and the Saints. Thus 53% knew that Jesus founded the Church. Only 28% knew that those who teach with full authority in the Church are the Pope together with the Bishops. Only 37% knew that Peter was named head of the Church by Jesus while 54% knew that the Pope is Vicar of Christ and head of the Universal Church. 42% had a correct notion of Ecumenism. Only 37% had the minimal knowledge of St. Paul. Even less, 30% knew who Saint John the Apostle was.

In most of the remaining thirteen questions on this category of the Church, the responses were better. Only two of the categories in this section showed rather significantly high percentages of correct answers. The two were on Mary as Mother of God and the definition of a pastor as the head of a parish.

RELIGIOUS TERMS

Religious Terms is another category where the young students seem to be confused, fuzzy and unsure. To illustrate: only 35% were aware of the meaning of Incarnation; 37% knew the meaning of the Immaculate Conception; 34% knew the meaning of Infallibility; 32% knew the role of the Pope; 49% were aware that Vatican II was a Council; 47% had a correct notion of Grace. On the positive side, of the remaining 21 questions, the majority were answered correctly. The students seemed extremely strong in their understanding of the term Sacraments and Original Sin.

SCRIPTURE

While the students manifested a greater knowledge of scriptures, much improvement is needed even in this most vital area. In spite of the expanded diversity of readings in the Sunday Liturgy, in spite of the constant emphasis of the Church on the need for scripture studies, the students failed to know some of the most basic facts, such as about Abraham, Moses, the Commandment of Jesus on love, St. Paul, St. John, the Humanity of Christ. Yet, they were very strong in their knowledge of Moses as receiving the Ten Commandments, the meaning of the Parable of the Prodigal Son and of the Good Samaritan. Again it can be said that except for the six weak areas, the majority scored quite well in the remaining 21 questions.

GOD

The responses improved in the category about God, His nature, Jesus and the Holy Spirit. The scores were very low only in 4 out of 20 questions. In these low scoring areas, the students indicated lack of knowledge that God reveals Himself through Jesus, the meaning of the Incarnation and the effect of the death and Resurrection of Christ. In most other areas, the respondents did rather well.

CHURCH LIFE

In the category of Church Life, Witness and Service, the knowledge increases significantly. In only 3 areas were there very poor responses. Thus, only 33% knew the purpose of canonizing Saints, 27% knew that Faith was a free gift of God, 24% knew that Jesus' great Commandment was to love God and Neighbor. There were two other areas on the nature of Grace as a gift of God in which the responses were 46% and 47% respectively. In the remaining 17 questions, the knowledge of the students was rather good.

SACRAMENTS

Probably because of the intense training for the reception of the Sacraments of Penance, Eucharist and Confirmation, the performance of the students excels in the area of the Sacraments. Out of 18 questions on the Sacraments, only one was below the 60%-70% range. Strangely, that one item showed that only 52% knew that Communion meant receiving Christ's actual Body and Blood sacramentally.

CONFRATERNITY OF CHRISTIAN DOCTRINE

In the table given above, the third column reflects the national average for the Parish Confraternity of Christian Doctrine program. While the C.C.D. students scored lower in each of the six categories, at the same time one must consider the various factors that would affect their scoring. They receive religious instruction for a very limited time in comparison to the Catholic Elementary School students. Frequently, their teachers are not trained as well as the teachers in the Catholic Schools. Furthermore, there is a greater tendency to view the C.C.D. program as a purely academic or educational program while religious training in the Catholic Schools has a better opportunity of being transmitted as a total religious experience.

When one looks at the scores for the C.C.D. program, one can only be encouraged that in spite of all the limitations and restrictions placed upon these students, they do rather well in their responses. In comparing the C.C.D. scores with those of the students in Catholic Schools, one should not ask why the C.C.D. students did more poorly than the Catholic School students but rather why did not the Catholic School students score significantly higher than the C.C.D. students.

The Diocese of Brooklyn did not conduct a survey of the C.C.D. program. However, one of the officials of the Diocesan Office of Catholic Education assured me that such a survey, if it had been carried out would probably match the national average just as the Catholic School average in the Diocese of Brooklyn practically equalled the national average.

2. 1980—R.E.O.I.—
Religious Attitudes Survey in Catholic Elementary Schools in the Diocese of Brooklyn

A separate, confidential section on Religious Attitudes of the 8th Grade elementary school students surveyed brought out significant insights into the impact of religious knowledge of the students on their interior life, attitudes and religious practices.

In 26 of the 40 inquiries made, the students manifested a relatively high degree of faith commitment and practice in their lives. This shows the beneficial effect of their training in the Catholic Schools in certain areas. However, even in this area of rather high commitment, one cannot but be surprised at the disbelief and doubts of so many. For example, while 75% believed Jesus is truly Divine and Human, one can only wonder why the remainder do not believe this or are not sure of the belief. 60% believe that following Jesus includes belonging to the Church, but 30% either disagree or are not sure of this truth. While 63% feel that people suffering from hunger are our concern, there is the significant percentage of 29% who do not believe this or are not sure.

The areas that showed the least impact of religious training on the conviction and life of the students are worth listing for they reflect the attitudes of the young and they present information which those involved in religious catechesis and in pastoral work cannot ignore:

1. 40% feel that some sins are too great for God to forgive or at least are not sure of this.
2. Only 14% held that the Holy Spirit guides Church leaders while 27% were not sure.
3. It was somewhat surprising to see that only 54% felt devotion to Mary was important in their lives and only 41% considered her an example of how they should live.
4. Only 40% believe that hell would be a punishment for a total rejection of God.
5. 41% either disagreed or were not sure that parents could help them about dating/sex.
6. Only 28% felt that religious teachers could be a source of advice on dating/sex.
7. Only 26% agreed that the Eucharist could help them whether they responded or not, while 71% disagreed or were not sure.
8. 42% felt that most of the time at Mass they were bored or distracted.
9. 44% either were not sure or believed that it was acceptable to get drunk as long as no one got hurt.
10. Only 58% considered it was wrong to lie in order to avoid trouble.
11. Only 17% felt that in the lives of priests, brothers, sisters, they found much that appealed to them.

3. 1980—R.E.K.A.P.—
Religious Knowledge Survey of Catholic High Schools in the Diocese of Brooklyn

In 1980, the Diocese of Brooklyn conducted a survey known as the Religious Education Outcomes of Knowledge, Attitudes and Practices (R.E.K.A.P.). This survey covered 395 students in the 11-12 grades in four different Catholic high schools.

The first section dealt with religious knowledge and covered the general areas of Church Doctrine, Church Life, Sacred Scripture and Religious Terms.

In only 13 of the 60 items did the students do rather poorly. The more significant of the items that fared poorly are the following:

1. 41% knew the effects of the Sacrament of the Anointing of the Sick.

2. 43% knew St. Paul as the Apostle to the Gentiles.

3. Only 32% considered that Catholic morality was an objective morality based on the nature of man. In fact, a noteworthy percentage (33%) felt that the Catholic position on morality meant that in every age, people created their own morality by free choice.

4. Only 39% answered correctly a common passage in scripture referring to the human nature of Christ.

5. Surprisingly only 36% answered correctly that the Church teaches that the source of gifts for the various ministries is the Holy Spirit, while 54% answered incorrectly that the Church teaches that the gifts have as their source the people themselves.

6. In the area of terminology, the students did very poorly in the meaning of such terms as Yahweh, infallibility, Ecumenism and Magisterium. In fact, one of the lowest percentages in the whole survey was that on Magisterium where only 24% could identify it.

It is very difficult to make any judgments on the results of such a survey. While the students seem to be somewhat weak in terminology and in certain areas of scripture, they seemed to do well in most areas of religious knowledge.

4. 1980—R.E.K.A.P.—
Religious Attitudes of Catholic High School Students in the Diocese of Brooklyn

The same Religious Education Outcomes Inventory Survey of the four Catholic high schools provided confidential information about the religious beliefs, attitudes and religious practices of the 11-12th grade students. Here again we have insights into the impact of their religious knowledge on their religious convictions, moral attitudes and religious practices.

The survey showed that the teachings of the Church seem to have little impact upon the beliefs in the Church's teachings on sexual activities such as birth control and pre-marital sex. There also seemed to be little impact of the Church's teaching on discrimination. Attendance at Mass likewise seemed to diminish among high school students.

Among the more significant responses in this area would be the following:

1. 31% felt that Jesus Christ was just a holy man, nothing more—or were not sure of their belief in this.

2. 49% believed that hell really exists while 15% felt that it did not exist and 36% were not sure.

3. 45% preferred to worship God in private prayer.

4. Only 40% believed that Christian lay people are called to holiness in the service of others no less than priests and Sisters.

5. Only 33% believed that the Church's position on birth control made sense while 38% disagreed and 29% were not sure.

6. 50% believed that for some couples, living together before deciding on marriage is the intelligent thing to do while 23% were not sure.

7. Only 41% accepted the Church as an important source of sound guidance on matters of sex and marriage. 25% did not accept the Church as sound guidance and 35% were not sure.

8. 39% believed that white people have a right to live in all-white neighborhoods if they so choose and that blacks must respect that right while 26% were not sure.

9. 32% believed that the birth of an unwanted child is worse than abortion while 22% were unsure and 47% disagreed.

10. Only 47% felt that religion answers questions about the meaning of life while 41% were unsure and 12% disagreed.

11. 32% either believed or were not sure there are private social activities from which one could in good conscience exclude certain people because of their race.

12. Only 27% believed that sexual intercourse outside of marriage is seriously wrong while 46% disagreed and 28% were not sure.

13. 53% attend Mass often while 21% attend occasionally, 23% seldom and 4% never.

II. Pastoral Problems of Catechesis

A. NATIONAL LEVEL

In 1977, the National Conference of Catholic Bishops submitted to the Secretariat preparing for the Synod on Catechesis in Rome a list of what it considered the major problems or obstacles affecting catechesis in the United States.[4] This list was the result of a survey of all the dioceses in our nation. The following would be a fair picture of the major problems of catechesis in the United States as reported not only in the survey of the National Conference of Catholic Bishops but also in other authoritative studies:

1. Dioceses identified as the most serious obstacle to catechesis the confusion, ambiguity, distrust, fear and even hostility and anger caused by a misunderstanding of the changes that have taken place in the wake of the Second Vatican Council. Religious education became one of the major battlegrounds for those who had opposing views on the Church and the world.

2. The confusion after Vatican Council II led to polarization which became an obstacle to religious education. Among the harmful aspects of the polarization was a rift between theologians and the Magisterium

resulting in teachers failing to make a clear distinction between theological opinion and what is taught by the Magisterium.

3. Difficulties with catechetical textbooks. Some complained of series that were "inaccurate, hurriedly written and foisted on the public" and were deficient in essential elements of doctrine and morality.

4. Lack of professionally trained teachers and catechists.

5. Lack of catechetical leadership and pastoral support on the part of Bishops and priests who abdicated their role as teachers, often turning over their responsibilities to others.

6. The American Bishops' Report listed several devastating problems which are not catechetical in origin or nature. The United States has been moving away from at least a semblance of allegiance to and practice of Christian values to the condition of a secularized and amoral society. Evidence of changes in the society are: the deterioration of the family, high divorce rate, one parent families, working mothers, increased juvenile delinquency, use of drugs, pornography, abortion, etc. The trend toward secularism has seriously impacted the Catholic Community.

7. In the area of non-catechetical obstacles, mention was also made of a dramatic increase of recreational and educational opportunities which compete with religious activities—notably religious education—with time and commitment. This affects all ages.

8. Loss of credibility in the Church's mission because of the resignation of many priests and religious from ministry.

9. One study listed as an obstacle "middle management" groups of theoreticians, publishers and even some teachers who effectually oppose full implementation of episcopal and papal teaching.[5]

10. Another study identified as a serious obstacle to catechesis the proliferation of ministries which is reducing the specialized mission of the Director of Education to

the status of one among many. With growing emphasis on the ministry of the family, the permanent diaconate, charismatic groups, parish ministry, youth ministry, ministry to the dying, aged, unchurched, divorced and separated Catholics and many others, a picture is developing of many ministries vying for the same population and all trying to establish their own turf.[6]

11. Failure to give priority to the involvement of the total family in the religious education program of the parish.

12. Failure to give priority to adult education in the parish. One study laments that while on the parish, diocesan and national level, there is much verbal support of adult education, the words are not noticeably translated into persons and structures. It feels that schools and CCD programs have priority over adult education and the Church is more child-oriented than adult-oriented.[7]

13. The estrangement of the youth from adults and from the mainstream of parish life.

14. The downgrading of parochial schools, depriving many children and youths of a sound and integrated religious formation.

15. The failure of an adequate catechetical program for handicapped persons.

16. Rejection of the Church as teacher on doctrinal and moral questions. Particularly is this true of the Church's credibility as moral teacher. Among the major reasons for this erosion are that people do not feel compelled to believe the Church when they disagree with it and secondly, the moral values of the laity are moving further from those advocated by the Church and towards the secularism of society. A corollary of this problem is the reality that, for most people, religion is on the backburner and not central in their lives.[8]

B. DIOCESE OF BROOKLYN

A survey on catechesis made in the parishes of the Diocese of Brooklyn in the Spring of 1981 resulted in a large response, particularly in this area of problems or obstacles affecting catechesis. The picture of the Diocese of Brooklyn is reflective to a large extent of that on the national level, as that on the national level is a good indicator of the state of catechesis in the Diocese of Brooklyn. Since this study of the Diocese of Brooklyn was made in preparation for this paper and is the most recent, I feel it would be very helpful to give a summary of its findings. Among the major problems that hinder catechesis in the Diocese of Brooklyn are the following:

1. Beyond all doubt, the most significant problem identified by the parishes is that of the lack of parental involvement in the catechetical formation of children. Parishes reported this as family or parental indifference, lack of interest, lack of faith and under many other terms. It all boils down to the fact that there is a woeful absence of parental support in the sacramental and religious life of the children. The responses listed more specific problems in this area of lack of parental support and the more important are worth noting:

    a. Separation of the family in the way we teach. Children are taught in one language, parents in another.

    b. Single parent families: widowed, divorced and separated, unwed.

    c. Unchurched parents who do not offer the sort of example that supports efforts of religious education programs.

    d. The neighborhood is very transitory so that parent formation does not have much time to affect people.

    e. Parents preoccupied with their own problems of economic subsistence, family problems, etc.

    f. Parents with closed minds to new approaches in teaching the Word of God.

    g. Unsophisticated, illiterate, foreign-speaking parents.

    h. Lack of parental presence in the home.

    i. Mixed marriage or divorced and remarried Catholics who do not seek baptism for children.

j. Insufficient basic knowledge on the part of parents results in little or no reinforcement of catechetical programs in the home.

k. Lack of parental discipline at home. Family problems.

l. Difficulty of relating religious language to real life experiences in the home. Example, God as a loving Father to a child when the father has abandoned the family or is an alcoholic.

m. Apathy on the part of parents for the child's spiritual and catechetical development.

n. Parents concerned only with instructions for the sacraments and not with the total catechetical formation of children.

o. Lack of faith at home with the resulting lack of attendance at Mass. Non-practicing Catholic parents who, however, insist that the children receive the sacraments. This causes confusion in the children.

p. Parents who are not solid, value-oriented models for their children.

q. Large numbers of families of mixed religion or non-Catholic single parents causing religious confusion within children.

2. The second largest identifiable problem was the lack of adult religious education programs. So many pointed out that the Church calls for priority being given to adult religious education programs but in actuality budget and personnel seemed to give the priority to children and youth ministries.

3. Apathy is listed as one of the most significant obstacles to catechesis. This apathy ranges across the whole spectrum of ages particularly among adults and parents. However, it does include children, youth and young adults. The apathy is manifested in poor attendance of children, youth and adults at Sunday Mass. It is also indicated by very poor attendance of public school children on the elementary and especially on the high school level at CCD classes. Programs offered for adult education are poorly attended. It must be admitted,

however, that a small percentage of this apparent apathy may actually be the inability to participate in religious activities because of the necessity of economic survival, language difficulties and other family problems.

4. Lack of catechetical leadership on the part of the pastor and lack of involvement by the other priests in the parish in the catechetical programs. It was indicated that some pastors have abdicated their leadership role as the one chiefly responsible for catechesis in the parish and handed it over to others. Lamented was the absence of priests from the Catholic School classroom and their failure to teach religion on some sort of regular basis in the school. At the same time, it was also stated that the clergy themselves lack the necessary education so that they can become an integral part of the religious education program. One parish reported that parents actually attend other Christian Churches because of the poor preaching on the part of the priests in their parish. In another parish, there was the problem of a deliberate exclusion of the pastor and priests from catechesis in the school by the Sister Principal.

5. One of the more significant problems identified was that of lack of complete unity in the teaching given to children, the young and adults, caused by indifference to the Magisterium of the Church. Confusion is caused by the dissemination of personal and so-called "expert" theological theories contrary to the official teachings of the Church. There was also a lament that devotion to the Blessed Mother is minimized in religious education. People have not been given a complete explanation of the changes in the Church. Another facet of the problem in this area is that there are conflicts on the theological and pastoral approaches of the pastor, assistants, religious and lay people. Another parish felt that there was a serious problem in the lack of proper instruction of all students in all articles of the Faith. More than one reported that many of the people, both young and adults,

do not know the major truths of the Catholic Faith. Correlated to this is a lack of knowledge of religious language and terminology.

6. Several parishes reported that one of the problems is the lack of clarity in the role description of the Religious Coordinator.

7. Several parishes reported obstacles which are not catechetical in nature, such as, that the parish is a changing, mobile one; poor living conditions resulting in a welfare mentality; the problem of evil present in the parish resulting in murders and other violence against people; the distance and transportation costs for over 50% of parishioners not within walking distance of the Church; the poverty of the people requiring them to work six days a week for minimal wages; low economic family problems lead to high mobility and hence work with families and individuals is so often incomplete.

8. One of the most common problems identified by the survey is that of the variety of cultural, racial, and language backgrounds of the parishioners. So many of the catechetical problems are caused by a large number of parents and even children who do not speak English and the woeful lack of clergy to speak their language. A corollary to this problem is the mixture of so many cultures in one parish and the inability to respond adequately to all the various cultural and language needs in the parish. A mixture of so many different racial and cultural groups creates also serious problems of prejudice among parishioners. One parish reported that the community is a very mobile community due to the presence of large numbers of undocumented aliens which makes sequence instruction and sacramental preparation almost impossible. Other parishes report the problem of the difference of outlook on the part of many recent immigrants with American ways and customs and their inability to adjust to these usages. As one person put it—so many of them are cultural Catholics as distinguished from Catholics. In areas dominated by Black population, there is a fear of the white middle class leaders in the parish. Another

similar parish reported that Blacks have special needs that we are not meeting although we try. In this particular area, there is the problem of lack of published catechetical materials geared for the various language and racial Catholic groups. In some parishes, there is an admitted lack of sensitivity to the various languages and cultures. At times, the parish staff is not always aware of ethnic groups in the parish. Where catechesis is given in the language of the people, this often creates an isolation of that group from the pastor and clergy who may not be able to speak the particular language.

9. A very large number of responses related to the problem of obtaining volunteer catechists. So many parishes admitted that volunteers are not in abundance. Those who do volunteer often do not have time to take courses for proper training. The problem of recruitment and training of catechists is considered by many as one of the most serious problems affecting the development of catechetical programs in the parish.

10. Also considered a serious problem in the parish is the lack of adequate professional training for parochial school teachers and religious education coordinators. Coupled with this is the lack of an ongoing formation program that would be spiritual, theological and pedagogical.

11. High among the problems reported by parishes is the high percentage of unchurched adults, youth and children who need evangelization even prior to catechization.

12. Lack of special catechetical education programs for the various handicapped persons: mentally retarded, deaf, physically disabled and with other disabilities.

13. One of the most serious problems presented by parishes is the lack of priority and guidance for CCD instruction. This is particularly a problem on the high school level. Some lament that too much attention is given to the Catholic School while so many of the children and young attend public schools. In this program of CCD, there is the repetition of the lack of parental sup-

port for the attendance of public school children at CCD classes. Coupled with the problem is the frustration that there is insufficient time in the CCD program to teach an extended curriculum to the public school students. There is also the related problem that in some parishes there is too sharp a distinction made between students in Catholic Schools and students in public schools. There is criticism of the difference in the amount of time and money expenditures per child for CCD and parochial school children in the parish. Some parishes have a complete absence of catechetical programs for public school children.

14. A large number of responses related to the textbooks on catechesis. The doctrinal content of the textbooks is considered weak by some and there is a call for a stronger curriculum of Catholic Dogma in the textbooks. Religion books do not review previously taught concepts. Another parish stated that most publishers of religious education textbooks assume that all the children come from good Catholic homes and that religion is taught in the home. Many school texts fail to give solid material for children to retain and to refer to. The lack of adequate content with solid teaching is lamented by a number of parishes. One response stated that the parish "would like to see publishers come out with books containing a lot more doctrine and less saccharin." There is the allegation that the current textbooks give theological and scriptural presentations which seem more preoccupied with forming just human beings rather than Christians. The phrase used several times is that textbooks fail to provide an adequate basic doctrinal formation and this results in a religious illiteracy.

15. Among other problems listed by parishes are the following:

    a. Alienation of adolescents and young people from the institutional Church.

    b. Lack of the total community involvement and cooperation in catechetical formation.

c. Lack of a total religious education program from the First Sacraments through adulthood.

d. A lack of proper integration of liturgy and catechesis. This problem particularly affects the Sunday liturgy.

e. Problems on the age for the reception of First Sacraments and the question of whether Penance should precede First Communion.

f. The difference among parishes in the area of policies for sacramental preparation.

III. Pastoral Achievements in Catechesis

A. NATIONAL LEVEL

A few studies and in particular the report of the National Conference of Catholic Bishops to the Synod Secretariat in Rome in 1977 demonstrate that not all is negative in the field of catechesis but that there are many positive achievements. Among the major pastoral achievements in catechesis on the national level are the following:

1. Successful programs for the sacramental preparation of children with parental involvement. This success centered largely around First Communion, First Penance and Confirmation. Admittedly there was less success with Baptism and, on an adult level, with Marriage.

2. A growth in teacher and catechist training programs on the national, diocesan and parish level.

3. Increase in youth ministry catechetical programs. While there were some catechetical progams for high school students that achieved a limited degree of success, it was admitted that there was widespread failure in reaching high school students.

4. A rapid increase in pre-school programs for catechesis of children between the ages of 3 and 5.

5. The priority given to total family catechesis.

6. A growth, though with limited success, of adult religious education programs.

7. A marked increase in the catechetical programs for the handicapped: physically, mentally, emotionally and with other disabilities.

8. Campus ministry programs are increasing in priority and achieving greater success.

9. Inclusion in catechesis of developments that have taken place in the fields of scripture, theology, liturgy, ecumenism and social doctrine.

10. The integration into catechetics of the findings of psychology, education, anthropology and sociology.

11. A balanced use of life experience as part of the method of catechesis.

12. Improved pedagogical methods.

13. With due allowance for shortcomings, there was encouragement for improvements in textbooks and media presentations in catechesis.

14. The growth in the number of professionally trained religious education coordinators and catechists.

15. Approval was given to the greater leadership role being assumed by women particularly in the field of religious education.

16. High praise was given to the greater involvement of the laity in the parish in catechetical programs either as members of Boards of Education in the parish or as catechists or in other areas in the field. As indicated above, particularly praiseworthy was the growing involvement of parents in the catechesis of their children, especially in preparation for the first reception of the sacraments.

17. The realization that catechesis is a lifelong process.

18. The developing awareness of the relationship of evangelization to catechesis.

19. The leadership and guidance role shown in church documents on catechesis, particularly three from the Holy See: the *General Catechetical Directory*, the

Apostolic Exhortation, *On Evangelization in the Modern World* of Pope Paul VI, the Apostolic Exhortation, *Catechesi tradendae* of Pope John Paul II; and three documents from the United States Hierarchy: The Pastoral Letter, *To Teach as Jesus Did,* the document, *Basic Teachings for Catholic Religious Education* and the *National Catechetical Directory.*

B. DIOCESE OF BROOKLYN

The results of the Spring 1981 survey made of the parishes in the Diocese of Brooklyn manifested a great deal of development in the field of catechesis. The amount of time, energy and commitment given by so many workers, particularly religious and laity, in this field prompts a feeling of great hope and encouragement. At the same time, the realistic awareness of widespread problems reminds us that there is so much more to be done. Once again the diocesan survey reflects that the positive developments in catechesis in the diocese reflect those on the national level, and those on the national level are generally similar to those of the Diocese of Brooklyn with certain local differences. The positive side of the picture of catechesis in the Diocese of Brooklyn can be seen from the following list of achievements gleaned from the survey:

1. In spite of a serious lack of parental involvement in catechetical programs for children especially in preparation for the First Sacraments, the largest number of positive responses centered on the growth of parental involvement in sacramental preparation of children. This held true in programs involving both parochial school students and CCD students. While on the national level there was very limited success in parental involvement in baptismal preparation programs, on the Brooklyn diocesan level this seemed to be one of the major successes. This program of parental involvement has had the benefit of the return of many unchurched parents to the practice of their Faith. It has also resulted in the establishment of

parent-teacher CCD associations and single parent groups. In baptismal preparation programs, parishes are also including not only parents but also godparents and other family members. The inclusion of the total family in the experience of the reception of the sacraments has been extended to preparation for First Penance, First Communion and Confirmation. This parental and family involvement in the sacraments is integrated with communal liturgical celebrations.

2. After parental and family involvement in catechetical programs, especially in preparation for the reception of the sacraments, the largest number of responses of a favorable nature centered on sacramental preparation in general. Noteworthy success is being achieved in many parishes in preparation for all of the sacraments. A large number mention successful pre-Cana programs in preparation for marriage. In both pre-Cana preparation and in preparation for Confirmation, several parishes mentioned the successful transfer of instructions to an in-home program. Preparations for the sacraments are carried out more frequently as parish celebrations. Preparations for the sacraments are integrated with appropriate liturgical celebrations. The sacramental teams involve the cooperation of all in the parish: priests, parochial school staff and CCD personnel. Several parishes indicated success in extending the preparation time for the sacraments of Penance, Eucharist and Confirmation. Some have extended them to two and three years and even more. Retreat days for those preparing for the sacraments of First Communion and Confirmation are becoming more frequent in parishes.

3. The third largest number of responses dealt with improvements in adult education programs. Many parishes admitted the priority of such programs. A significant number of parishes are beginning to initiate programs for the divorced and separated. Adult planning boards have been established to implement programs in the parish. A variety of adult instruction programs have been initiated. Some have adult instructions once a week

for ten months of the year. Some have home visitation programs. Others indicated that the Genesis II and Romans VIII programs have been very successful. Still others have begun to form senior citizen programs of religious instruction. Several parishes mention the need for evangelization of so many unchurched and alienated adults. Several parishes noted the success of the adult catechumenate program carried out in accordance with the Rite of Christian Initiation for Adults. A number of parishes link the adult education programs with the liturgical cycle, particularly during Advent and Lent. Significant success has been achieved in adult minicourses in the study of the Bible and liturgy. One parish indicated that private instructions are given to adults where the desire is expressed. Other parishes combine in their programs prayer, religious instruction and discussion. Many parishes indicate that the adult education programs are given in the languages of the people when they cannot speak English. Single adult programs are also increasing in number in parishes.

4. The next most notable achievement boasted by parishes is the increased number of religious education coordinators and catechists who have received professional training. Many parishes indicated that the success of their catechetical programs depends largely on the professionalization and ongoing education of their catechists and religious education coordinators. Prominent in the responses was the necessity of the achievement of certification by catechists. Also emphasized as essential is the spiritual formation of the catechists and religious coordinators. Several parishes noted that the faculty and staff of CCD programs and also of teachers and administrators in the Catholic School participate in retreat days and prayer sessions.

5. The integration of catechesis and liturgy was identified by a large number of parishes as a notable success. Communal Penance services during Lent and Advent were considered a positive achievement. The conducting of catechetical programs during Lent and Advent

was a frequent occurrence in parishes. In parishes, greater attention is being given to music as an element in catechesis. Monthly family liturgies are celebrated in some communities. In the parish school, school liturgies and para-liturgies at various times of the school year have proved rewarding for both students and faculty. "Liturgy of the Word" groups composed of students from both the parochial and public schools have proved beneficial.

6. Considered a great benefit is the increase in number of volunteer catechists who not only teach religious education but also by their practice of their Faith set a good example for their students.

7. While CCD programs have shown that a large number of elementary and public high school students are not being reached, nevertheless, many parishes feel that this is a necessary program which has achieved a marked degree of success. Some have classes for public school children on Mondays and Wednesdays. An increasing number of parishes are changing the released time classes from Wednesday afternoon to Sundays immediately after Mass, finding that this is a more appropriate time both for the students and for the teachers. Other parishes conduct sessions on Saturdays and have found success in this time slot. Another parish mentioned successful CCD programs for high school students in the evening and indicated that it has its own security force. Any success due to the CCD programs is due to parental involvement and the dedication of the volunteer faculty and staff. Also considered an important quality for success of CCD programs is the integration of instruction and policy between the Catholic School and the CCD process.

8. Catechesis for children is listed among the highest successes of parish programs. An increasing number of parishes are conducting pre-school programs involving children between the ages of 3 to 5. Parishes are noting a significant increase in parochial school registration. Small parishes are conducting weekly Sunday School of Reli-

gion classes for pre-school, kindergarten and first-grade children. Special liturgies are conducted for children at certain times through the year.

9. Several parishes noted that the success of their catechetical programs flowed from the excellent cooperation and rapport between the clergy in the parish and the school teachers, religious coordinators, and catechists. They mention that the leadership role of the pastor and priests is still most important for a successful catechetical program. Considered important, though not listed frequently, was the benefit of priests themselves teaching religion in the schools on a regular basis. In the diocese, as in the nation, there seems to be a lessening of the polarization between clergy and religious education teachers and catechists that characterized the 60's.

10. Evangelization programs under various names, such as "Homecoming," were considered creative innovations and successes.

11. Many parishes listed positive achievements in religious instructions in the various languages of the people of their parishes. Some parishes conduct trilingual liturgies, particularly on special feast days. Among the Spanish, there is a great interest in the Cursillos and Cursillo related programs. There is a growing understanding and sensitivity to the language and cultures of the different peoples of parishes particularly when conducting liturgies and instruction programs. Pre-Cana, Bible classes and various other instructional programs are given in various languages.

12. There is increased attention being given to catechetical programs for the handicapped of all ages and of various disabilities. One parish indicated the success of an ongoing spiritual formation of parents of handicapped persons. The Diocese itself has a very successful diocesan program coordinating sacramental preparation, religious instruction and liturgies for the handicapped.

13. A number of parishes singled out as a positive benefit the growth of the parish as a faith community. Achievement of a faith community awareness is seen by

some as the product of the parish community involving itself directly in catechetical programs.

14. Numerous parishes listed as one of the most important achievements in the success of their catechetical programs the hiring of a full time, professionally trained Religious Education Coordinator, or Youth Minister, or CCD Coordinator.

15. A few parishes indicated as an achievement the development of service projects enabling students and those preparing for the sacraments to practice Christian service. One parish established a social service agency to reach out to troubled and needy families. Since such service programs are witnessing to Christian values they are considered part of catechetical programs.

16. Youth ministry is also singled out as one of the more important achievements in the pastoral ministry of the parish even though there is the admission of widespread lack of success in reaching the young and young adults. Several parishes have established teen clubs and programs and have found success in them. The purpose of these youth programs is to continue catechesis for post-Confirmation students. Several parishes conduct small discussion groups of high school students. Other parishes have established youth discipleship programs. In one parish the teen program is conducted on a one-to-one basis through the parish center.

IV. Observations, Priorities and Recommendations

The Apostolic Exhortation, *Catechesi tradendae*, contains the most recent synthesis of the general principles that presently can serve as an authentic, authoritative guide to effective catechesis. It is not my task to repeat the principles so clearly set down in *Catechesi tradendae* and in the other authoritative sources. In this final section I shall present some of the major observations, priorities and recommendations which, in the light of the present state of catechetics in this nation and in the Diocese of Brooklyn, might serve as a partial aid in the implementation of an effective catechesis.

A. OBSERVATIONS ON REJECTION OF THE CHURCH AS TEACHER BY THE YOUNG

The National Opinion Research Center/Knights of Columbus Study presented by Professor McCready along with other studies more than indicate that young people have rejected the Church as teacher. This is a grave problem for the Church as a whole and not just for Catholic catechists and educators. The studies in the Diocese of Brooklyn reflect a most interesting fact. A high percentage of our students seems to *know* well what the Church teaches. However, the percentage which *accepts* this teaching is much smaller. This leads to two observations:

1. The problem is not knowledge; it is faith. It seems that we have a subtle form of gnosticism operating today which expresses itself in the observation: "We are not teaching our children what the Church teaches; if we did teach them, then obviously they would accept it." This position falsely identifies faith with knowledge. At the same time, it must be remembered that faith and knowledge are closely related, for true knowledge of the Catholic Faith is essential. The basic problem we have is a pastoral one: how does one nourish the growth of *faith* among young people who live in a culture that is openly hostile to the teachings of the Church? This is the primary pastoral challenge facing religious catechists and educators today. There is the fear, however, that the unconscious gnostics in our midst propose means of solving this problem that are more educational than pastoral. In fact, both approaches must be utilized.

2. My second observation is that I believe we have a difficult problem struggling with the apathy in the

Church community toward religious catechesis in general. When the NORC study presented by Dr. McCready indicated that 73% of public high school youngsters did not have any religious instruction, one must note the reasons that he gave: no interest in religion, their friends are not going, their parents do not care, they already know enough religion. All of these reasons are forms of apathy. While Professor McCready gave statistics only for public high school students, I have no doubt that the problem affects a large percentage of those attending Catholic Schools.

3. The problem of apathy is a pastoral one and a leadership one. Little direction has been given to parish leadership on how to handle the difficulties of developing faith in a hostile community. As one very knowledgeable Catholic educator informed me, religious educators have been in many instances serious obstacles for parish leaders precisely because they have been out of touch—and at times out of line—with Church teaching. He felt that the hierarchy, not knowing how to deal with the problem, has devoted too much energy to the important social ministry of the Church where they felt more comfortable. If the Church through its pastoral leaders does not give more attention to this religious education problem soon, we will have a Church that is socially active, but devoid of any doctrinal basis for its existence.

B. OBSERVATIONS ON THE RELATIONSHIP OF CATECHESIS AND LITURGY

Constantly emphasized in recent documents on catechesis is the principle that no pastoral ministry can be carried out in isolation from the others. The pastoral activities of Word, Worship and Service are intertwined and represent three aspects of the one pastoral mission of Christ and of the Church. This cooperation and even dependence in pastoral ministry must exist also between catechesis and liturgy, not only in theory but also in practice.

While all the documents, including *Catechesi tradendae*, the *General Catechetical Directory*, and the *National Catechetical Directory* call for a cooperation between catechists and liturgists, and while on the structural level there is a rather close collaboration between the Federation of Diocesan Liturgical Commissions, the National Conference of Diocesan Directors of Religious Education and the Bishops' Commission on the Liturgy, there still exist today a certain latent hesitancy, suspicion and differences between catechists and liturgists on the local level. This represents a problem in the pastoral mission of the diocese and of the parish, a problem which hopefully will be resolved in time.

A common allegation made by liturgists is that catechists are abusing the liturgy and creating disorder in it. Catechists frequently regard liturgy as being so rubrical that it is meaningless and, in fact, is at times contrary to what catechesis is trying to achieve.

The problem is that often catechists are put in the position of being liturgists, frequently because liturgists will not work together with catechists to prepare the liturgies. In attempting to make the liturgy more meaningful, catechists naturally will use catechetical rather than liturgical elements. For example, the catechesis on Confirmation becomes centered on the social aspect rather than on the action of the Holy Spirit, and the celebration of Confirmation becomes the affirmation of what has been achieved rather than allowing the Spirit to produce its effects. In addition, catechists at times may have little confidence in the power of liturgical symbols and more confidence in pedagogy and the process of education. There is the temptation to make the liturgy an educational tool which is often less than totally effective since it violates the symbolic genre of liturgy.

Another problem facing catechists is that within catechesis today there is an emphasis on God communicating Himself as a person. Catechists often find it hard to bring this emphasis to life in a liturgy that is sometimes very word heavy, conceptual and somewhat restrictive. Catechists sometimes feel that liturgists do not understand that catechesis wants to produce a liturgy that promotes a vibrant faith life. Oftentimes catechists feel that poor liturgical celebrations kill the very life that they are trying to nourish.

A clearer perspective on these and other problems that may exist between liturgists and catechists could be hoped for if we realized that catechesis and liturgy are two ministries on the same level existing not to be in conflict but to work together in helping to bring to life a deep faith shared in common. Some help might be offered by a few of the ideas which Albert Rouet contributed in a 1979 article.[9] He and other authors, such as Father David N. Power[10] and Father John Gurrieri,[11] are urging that much of the tension in the relationship between liturgy and catechesis can be lessened if more attention were paid to the Church's emphasis on evangelization and especially on the Rite of Christian Initiation of Adults.

Rouet points out a few areas of difficulty between liturgy and catechesis. Liturgy proceeds within a yearly cycle which then repeats itself. Catechesis usually works within a school cycle which then fits into a program which is ongoing over a number of years. The catechist is more sensitive to synchronization. There is no simple statement. The cultural, political and social aspect of problems have to be considered and incorporated. History, art, current events all impact on people and things. Liturgy is seen as being diachronic or relating to phenomena as they occur over a period of time. Liturgy gives itself time to see and has more of an evolutionary dimension to it. Liturgy is interested in fidelity to its origins and has a high respect for the age and continuity of its rights. Catechesis, on the other hand, communicates a content that is at the same time continuous and yet in a certain sense broken with the change of political, social, cultural events.

The author points out that another difficulty is with the Word of God. Both liturgy and catechesis see the Word of God as normative. Liturgy allows the Word of God to be presented, but at the same time allows that Word to emerge and become real now. The yesterday of the Word becomes the today of its proclamation. Catechesis is more sensitive to the context which surrounds the proclamation. The new methods of exegesis, joined to new methods of reading and analyzing texts, oblige the catechist to a certain restraint toward the symbolic use of the Word. For the catechist, liturgy does not suffice when it simply exposes or proclaims the Word.

Rouet and other authors feel that the solution to the tensions is not that liturgy and catechesis should lose their identity. Both can discover the road ahead together by looking more closely at evangelization.

The one thing that is certain about the future of catechesis and liturgy is that they will realize their need for each other. It is a need that was reflected from the very beginnings of the Church. In the early centuries of the Church, catechesis and liturgy were so related that they were not even distinguishable from one another. In fact, in the first five centuries, all catechesis took place through liturgical experiences: the liturgy, the homily during the liturgy, the unfolding of the liturgical year.

While today, as has been indicated, there is a remnant of a discordance between liturgist and catechist, we are witnessing a closer relationship between catechesis and liturgy in which one does not become the tool of the other but rather in which both realize that they seek the same goal—the conversion and illumination of the faithful in the Word of God, the Worship of and Prayer to God, and the Service of all to others.

In a paper submitted to the Synod of Bishops in Rome by the United States National Conference of Catholic Bishops, the author emphasized the close collaboration that must exist between catechesis and liturgy: "Because it leads individuals and communities to deeper faith, all catechesis is oriented to prayer and worship.

The deepening of faith strengthens the covenant relationship with God and calls Christians to respond in worship and ritual.... Catechesis promotes active, conscious participation in the liturgy. It reminds us that, whether at times we feel like praying or not, liturgical prayer, like all prayer, is as necessary for spiritual life as are water and bread for physical life."[12]

The central importance of a cooperation between catechesis and liturgy in pastoral ministry is one of the major thrusts of the *National Catechetical Directory* for the United States. Herein we find the principle of cooperation which must be the essence of all pastoral activities in our dioceses and parishes. The *Directory* reminds us:

> There is a close relationship between catechesis and liturgy. Both are rooted in the Church's faith, and both strengthen faith and summon Christians to conversion, although they do so in different ways. In the liturgy the Church is at prayer, offering adoration, praise, and thanksgiving to God, and seeking and celebrating reconciliation; here one finds both an expression of faith and a means for deepening it. As for catechesis, it prepares people for full and active participation in liturgy (by helping them understand its nature, rituals and symbols) and at the same time flows from liturgy, inasmuch as, reflecting upon the community's experiences of worship, it seeks to relate them to daily life and to growth in faith.[13]

As one author picturesquely put it: "The focus of catechesis is not the classroom but the chapel."[14]

C. PRIORITIES AND RECOMMENDATIONS

1. Highest priority, I am convinced, must be given to the contents of catechesis. If one of the major goals of catechesis is to bring the individual and the community to a faith-filled, intimate union with Jesus Christ, then the faithful must know Jesus. They must know the truth, the

whole truth and nothing but the truth about who Jesus Christ is, what He is and what He taught. Love and service of God are products of our faith-knowledge of God. The nature and direction of our love and service will largely depend on our faith-knowledge. It bears repeating that the extent of religious knowledge does not necessarily or automatically lead to a faith commitment. But a faith commitment does require knowledge of religious truths.

In the plan of God, the truth about Christ and Christ's teaching reaches us through the Catholic Church and, in particular, through its Magisterium. It is the orthodox teaching of the Church's Magisterium that must be transmitted and made alive in the process of bringing people to a greater union with Jesus Christ. The aim of catechesis is to make the Catholic Faith active, living and conscious and to nourish and mature that faith so that the person and the community will live in and for God. With such an aim, there is no room for theological confusion and ambiguity. There is no place for dissenting opinions or so-called "reputable" theologians presented as having equal or at least probable authority with the Church's Magisterium. Contradictory theological opinions may have their proper place in religious education as an academic and research enterprise, but catechesis is not solely an academic activity. It is much more. It is a living, salvation-oriented activity of the Church in accordance with the teachings and laws of the Church. Whatever is contrary to the teachings and laws of the Church is contrary to the nature and goals of catechesis.[15]

2. An adjunct to the priority of the Church's Magisterium is the pivotal role of the Bishop as chief catechist. This primary mission of the Bishops was enunciated in Vatican Council II and reinforced in *Catechesi tradendae* and in other catechetical documents.

The Bishops of this country should continue an effective dialogue with theologians, some of whom proclaim teachings contrary to those of the Church. The aim of this dialogue is to remove what amounts to a double

Magisterium. So often today, the speculative opinions of some theologians have greater impact on what is taught in catechetical programs than the teachings of the Church.

The Bishops of this country and the Bishop in his diocese must determine what is authentic and orthodox teaching. This requires that the Bishop become more personally involved in the preparation, execution, and evaluation of catechetical programs in his diocese. His right and obligation as chief teacher of doctrine and morals must remain intact juridically and actually.

3. As associates of the Bishop in his role as the chief teacher and catechist, pastors and priests in parishes must effectively carry out their function as guardians and teachers of the truth in their parish. This will require on their part a greater personal direction and supervision of catechetical programs in their community. Catechesis is a pastoral priority of the Church and of the priests. The control of this essential mission of the Church cannot be abdicated to others though its implementation requires the services of many others. This retention of his function as guardian of the teachings of the Church in his parish does not imply that the pastor should not seek and utilize the input and services of professional religious coordinators, catechists, and teachers. All must cooperate as an harmonious unit in achieving a successful catechesis of the total community. However, the ultimate responsibility on the parish level must remain with the pastor and priests, as on the diocesan level it rests with the Bishop.

4. A major priority for an effective pastoral catechesis is the presence of a professionally trained religious coordinator and/or catechist. The success of catechetical programs in parishes seems directly linked to these persons. The positive achievement of these trained catechists and of their programs is significantly increased where there is cooperation with all the other leadership persons in the parish: clergy, school administrators and faculty, CCD Coordinators, Youth Ministers, etc.

Important also is the continuing education of catechists in doctrine, methods, etc. In order to provide the necessary training and degrees, there is an increased call for the establishment on the diocesan and national level of accredited and well-staffed catechetical institutes that would provide orthodox catechetical and spiritual formation for catechists.

An essential requirement that must be emphasized is the spiritual formation of catechists. Many have stated that more important is what a catechist is than what a catechist teaches. The catechist cannot be solely a conveyor of knowledge. He or she must be primarily a witness of Jesus Christ.

5. In the area of contents, greater importance must be given to the textbooks and other materials used as instruments of catechetical instruction. Basic is that they contain orthodox teaching. However, they must also be adequate pedagogically and educationally, that is, they must be adapted to the ages, conditions, backgrounds and ethnic cultures of the students. Today textbooks and materials often fail to take sufficient consideration of the multiple cultural backgrounds of the faithful.

The catechetical textbooks and materials often fail to appreciate the realities of the economic, social and moral conditions of family life in our urban areas where divorce, separation, unmarried parents, sexual permissiveness, poverty, child abuse, alcoholism, drug abuse, etc., impact so many of our young. Concepts of father, mother, family of God, love of parents, etc., evoke quite different emotions and reactions than those expected from the use of such terms in many catechetical textbooks and materials.

6. In the category of implementation of pastoral catechesis, the first priority enunciated by almost all studies is the participation of parents in the faith maturation of the child. This participation of the parents takes on various forms. It calls for parents themselves to receive catechesis, to become personally involved in the sacramental preparation of children, to be models of the

Catholic Faith for their children, to create a spirit of prayer and faith in the family, to participate in the pastoral life of the parish community.

7. Another priority intimately linked with parental involvement is adult education. This is often verbally termed the first priority, though it is lamented that the words are not translated into actual programs. Adult catechesis must incorporate and adapt to the religious growth of adults of all ages and conditions: married, single parents (divorced, separated, widowed, unwed), handicapped, young, senior citizens, etc. Within this sphere is also the obligation of adults to participate more actively in the total pastoral ministry of the parish wherever they are needed. Only the laity, under the leadership of the priests and other catechetical personnel, can make the parish a faith-community.

8. In many urban areas particularly, such as in the Diocese of Brooklyn, priority must be given to the adaptation of catechetical programs to the multi-lingual, multi-cultural, multi-racial complexus of the parishes. As in all other conditions of the people, so in this, we must take people where they are at. We must catechize in their language when they cannot be instructed in English. We must be sensitive to the history and culture of their countries and racial backgrounds.

In addition, the Church, as part of this catechetical ministry, must develop in the faithful a realization that newcomers to our community are our brothers and sisters and should be welcomed as such. In the Kingdom of God there are no aliens.

9. Throughout the country there is a growing number of unchurched. So often what is urgent in our parishes is not catechesis which builds on the initial acceptance of the Faith but the prior step of evangelization. In so many dioceses, there is a large number of baptized adults and children who are unaware of even the rudiments of the Faith. Recommended highly is the excellent program of the Rite of Christian Initiation of

Adults, a highly successful program though presently infrequently implemented.

10. In spite of occasional contrary voices, self-proclaiming is the priority that must continue for the traditional catechesis given through the maintenance of our Catholic Schools and CCD Programs. Greater attention should be given to a more viable cooperation between the Catholic School and the CCD Programs. CCD Programs, as evidenced in several studies, are not reaching a large segment of the public school students and call for creative, aggressive programs.

11. Youth Ministry is still one of the most important pastoral activities of the parish. The loss of so many youth and young adults is an occasion of widespread frustration among clergy and catechists, not to mention parents. So many forces are combatting the value system of the Church—whether it be television, movies, pornography, sexual permissiveness, drugs, alcoholism, secularism, peer pressure, doctrinal confusion, consumerism, etc. These forces of evil are powerful but the grace of God is even more powerful. The Church through its clergy, religious and faithful must be hopeful that it can influence the youth and bring them closer to God. This hope, however, must be fleshed out with energetic and innovative pastoral activities.

12. A growing realization is the need of increased and specialized catechesis of the handicapped of various disabilities as well as specialized catechesis of their parents and families.

13. Highest probably in the amount of time and energy given by parish catechetical staff leaders is the sacramental preparation of children for Penance, First Communion and Confirmation. This priority should continue. The programs should constantly be evaluated. Sacramental preparation should always be utilized as an occasion for parental and family involvement and catechesis. This holds not only for the sacraments mentioned above but also for Baptism and Marriage.

14. As mentioned in another context, it is essential that catechesis always take people where they are at. An implication of this principle is the recognition that the life-experiences of people are an important factor to be addressed and incorporated in an effective catechesis.

15. Among the most significant realities of pastoral ministry is the often neglected principle that no pastoral ministry can be independent of the others. All ministries are facets of the one goal of the Church—the salvation of souls. In a special way, as elaborated above, must this principle be implemented through an increased integration of catechesis and the liturgical life of the parish. The Word of God in catechesis must join the Worship of God in the liturgy. Liturgy and catechesis, while neither can be a tool of the other, must directly cooperate in achieving the mission of the Church.

16. Catechesis must keep in mind that growth in faith by the individual and by the community must overflow into the love of neighbor. This love of neighbor must be actualized through service to others in programs of aid to the poor and needy, activities on behalf of social justice, etc. In short, the corporal works of mercy are an essential goal of catechesis, or perhaps better, an excellent sign of the effectiveness of catechetical programs. On several occasions, the Church has stated authoritatively that programs on behalf of social justice are a constitutive dimension of the gospel message.

17. There is an increasing recognition that the Church in the United States must develop a greater and more imaginative use of communication and various communication media in its catechetical mission. If the Church is failing to reach so many, perhaps it is in the electronic field of communication and other media that it may achieve greater success.

18. In the preparation and implementation of catechetical programs, there is a necessity of cooperation among neighboring parishes in urban areas as well as a sharing of information on catechetical programs among all parishes in the diocese. The increased costs of main-

taining facilities, the salaries for personnel as well as the decrease in the number of clergy are additional reasons for the self-evident benefits of cooperation and sharing of data on catechesis.

19. Both teachers and parents are calling for a balanced utilization of memorization as a pedagogical tool in catechesis. Understanding and interiorization of Faith is essential but appropriate memorization has its benefits also. There are widespread complaints that children do not know a simple Act of Contrition, the Hail Mary, the Our Father, the Ten Commandments and the meaning of some basic terms of our Faith.

20. Evaluation of catechetical programs is a process that needs little elaboration. Only by honest and scientific evaluation can there be development in catechesis through the elimination of the useless, maintenance or expansion of the successful, adaptation in changing conditions, creation of new approaches, etc. Results of evaluation should be shared with other parishes and interested diocesan agencies.

21. Most essential in the pastoral ministry of catechesis is the encouragement and support that should be given to religious catechists. They often face great frustration and even fears. With a spirit of Christian dedication, they expend energy and time, often without adequate material recompense. The whole Church, through its Pope, Bishops, priests, religious and faithful, owes to the catechists an expression of appreciation and gratitude that cannot be enlarged or repeated enough. While much remains to be done in catechesis, much has been achieved. The religious state of our nation, of our diocese, of our parishes may not be at its best but imagine what it would be without our catechetical programs.

22. As the last but most necessary priority in catechesis, I quote the response of one priest in answer to the diocesan survey. He put the highest priority in one word: *Pray.*

FOOTNOTES

1. *Catechesi tradendae*, no. 20.
2. *General Catechetical Directory*, nos. 14, 21.
3. *Catechesis: Realities and Visions*. (1977 Symposium on Catechesis of Children and Youth), United States Catholic Conference, Washington, D.C., pp. 10-18. (Includes summary of four studies commissioned and published by the United States Catholic Conference: *Where Are the 6.6 Million*, by Wilfred H. Paradis and Andrew D. Thompson, 1976; *The Next 15 Years*, by Andrew D. Thompson, Che-fu Lee and Wilfred H. Paradis, 1976; *Religion and American Youth*, by Raymond H. Potvin, Dean R. Hoge and Hart M. Nelson, 1976; *The Religious Children*, by Hart M. Nelson, Raymond H. Potvin and Joseph Shields, 1977.)
4. "The State of Catechesis in the United States." (Report of the National Conference of Catholic Bishops to the Synod Secretariat.) *Origins*, April 21, 1977, Vol. 6, no. 44, pp. 705-708; April 28, 1977, Vol. 6, no. 45, pp. 718-724.
5. Rev. Michael J. Wrenn, "Religious Education at the Crossroads," *Faith and Reason*, VI, no. 4, Winter 1980, p. 297.
6. Rev. Eugene Hemrick, "The Identity of the Parish Religious Education Director," *Dimensions of Ministry*, January-February 1980, Vol. 2, no. 3, p. 12.
7. "Diocesan Adult Education Directors," *Position Papers and Recommendations from the Symposium on the Parish and the Educational Mission of the Church*. Department of Education, United States Catholic Conference, 1977, p. 14; Anne Marie Mongovern, "The Directory: A Word for the Present," *The Living Light*, Vol. 16, no. 2, Summer 1977, pp. 143-144.
8. Raymond H. Potvin, "Research, Theory and Practice in Religious Education: A Triadic Bond," *Catechesis: Realities and Visions*, Department of Education, United States Catholic Conference, 1977, p. 25.
9. Albert Rouet, "Catechese et Liturgie: Radiographie d'un de bat Insuffisant," *La Maison-Dieu*, no. 140, 1979, pp. 7-23.
10. David N. Power, "The Mystery Which Is Worship," *The Living Light*, Vol. 16, no. 2, 1979, pp. 168-178.
11. Rev. John A. Gurrieri, "Liturgy and Catechesis: Renewing an Old Friendship," *Dimensions of Ministry*, Department of Education, United States Catholic Conference, pp. 20-24.
12. "The Catechist as a Teacher of Prayer," (Paper Submitted to 1977 Synod of Bishops by National Conference of Catholic Bishops), *Origins*, October 27, 1977, Vol. 17, no. 17, p. 303.
13. *National Catechetical Directory*, no. 113.
14. Michael Warren, "Catechesis: An Enriching Category for Religious Education." *Religious Education*, Vol. 76, no. 2, March-April 1981, p. 123.
15. *National Catechetical Directory*, no. 47.

BIBLIOGRAPHY

Boys, Mary C., S.N.J.M., "The Standpoint of *Religious Education*," Religious Education, Vol. 76, no. 2, March-April 1981, pp. 128-141.

Brown, Raymond E., S.S., "Difference of Thought as a Constructive Christian Force—A Biblical View." Paper given at 78th Convention of NCEA, N.Y.C., April 22, 1981.

Campbell, Anna S., "Toward a Systematic Catechesis: An Interpretation of *Catechesi Tradendae,*" *The Living Light,* Vol. 17, no. 4, Winter 1980, pp. 311-320.

Pope John Paul II, *Catechesi tradendae,* Apostolic Exhortation on Catechetics, October 25, 1979. English Translation in *Origins,* November 8, 1979, Vol. 9, no. 21, pp. 330-347.

Catechesis: Realities and Visions. A Symposium on the Catechesis of Children and Youth. Ed. by Marianne Sawicki and Berard L. Marthaler, Publications Office, United States Catholic Conference, 1977.

"The Catechist as a Teacher of Prayer." Paper submitted to 1977 Synod of Bishops by NCCB. *Origins,* October 27, 1977, Vol. 17, no. 17, pp. 302-303.

The Catholic School. Sacred Congregation for Catholic Education, March 19, 1977, Publications Office, United States Catholic Conference, 1977.

Critical Issues. A Revised Report on the Work of the Adult Education Regional Consultants, September 1979, Department of Education, United States Catholic Conference.

Dooley, Catherine, O.P., "Catechesis in Our Time," *Louvain Studies,* Vol. 7, 1979, pp. 145-204.

Forliti, John E., "Catechesis and Youth Ministry," from *Catechesis: Realities and Visions,* pp. 109-119.

Funk, Mary Margaret and DeBoy, Jr., James J., "DRE's and School Principals: Partners in Ministry," *Pace 22,* 1981, Community-H, pp. 1-5.

Frye, Mariella, M.H.S.H., "Reflections on the National Catechetical Directory for the United States and the Roman Synod in Catechetics in Our Times," *Louvain Studies,* Vol. 7, 1979, pp. 205-211.

Geoghegan, Sister Theophane, "Parish Catechesis Today," *The Month,* November 1979, pp. 375-378.

"Going, Teach...," Commentary on the Apostolic Exhortation, *Catechesi tradendae,* of John Paul II, St. Paul Editions, Boston, 1980.

Griese, Rev. Orville, "The Pastor's Role in Religious Education," *Homiletic and Pastoral Review,* LXXIX, no. 3, December 1978, pp. 65-71.

Gurrieri, Rev. John A., "Liturgy and Catechesis: Renewing an Old Friendship," *Dimensions of Ministry,* Department of Education, United States Catholic Conference, November/December 1980, pp. 20-24.

Hofinger, Johannes, "Evangelization in the Catechesis of Children," *The Living Light,* Vol. 12, no. 2, 1975, pp. 213-219.

Iannone, Joseph and Mercedes, "Family Learning Team Approach to Total Parish Education," *Pace 11,* 1980, Community-A, pp. 1-5.

Jewitt, Bernard C., "The Parish and Its Influence on the Religious Education of Youth," from *Catechesis: Realities and Visions,* pp. 54-56.

John Paul II, Catechist. Text with Commentary on *Catechesi tradendae,* Franciscan Herald Press, Chicago 1978.

Lebeau, Paul and Charytanski, Jan, "The Fifth Synod of Bishops and the Church's Catechetical Mission," *Lumen Vitae,* Vol. XXXIII, no. 1, 1978, pp. 19-36.

Marthaler, Berard L., "Defining While Not Defining—The Paradox of the National Directory," *Pace 9,* 1978, pp. 1-3.

Marthaler, Berard L., "What Is the Ministry of a DRE?" *The Living Light,* XIV, no. 4, Winter 1977, pp. 511-518.

McCready, William C., "Catholic Schools and Catholic Youth, Commitment and Community." A Report on the NORC/Knights of Columbus Research Study. Presented to 78th Annual Convention of NCEA, N.Y.C., April 20-23, 1981.

Melchert, Charles F., "What Is Religious Education?" *The Living Light,* Vol. 14, no. 3, Fall 1977, pp. 339-353.

"Message to the People of God," from the World Synod of Bishops, *Origins,* November 10, 1977, Vol. 7, no. 21, pp. 321-328.

Meyers, Rev. John F., "Developments Since the Pastoral [To Teach as Jesus Did]: An Educational Perspective," *Notre Dame Journal of Education*, Vol. 6, Fall 1975, no. 3, pp. 205-210.

Miller, Randolph Crump, "Some Clarifying Thoughts About Religious Education," *The Living Light*, Vol. 13, no. 4, 1976, pp. 487-498.

Mongovern, Anne Marie, "The Directory: A Word for the Present," *The Living Light*, Vol. 16, no. 2, Summer 1979, pp. 135-148.

Murdick, Msgr. Olin J., "Developments Since the Pastoral [To Teach as Jesus Did]: A Pastoral Perspective," *Notre Dame Journal of Education*, Vol. 6, Fall 1975, no. 3, pp. 107-204.

"National Conference of Diocesan Directors: Goals and Objectives 1979-1982," *Dimensions of Ministry*, Department of Education, United States Catholic Conference, Vol. 1, no. 4, Summer 1979, pp. 16-19.

Nelson, C. Ellis, "Trends in Society and Culture Related to the Catechesis of Youth," from *Catechesis: Realities and Visions*, pp. 27-35.

Nichols, Kevin, "Scope and Nature of Religious Education," *The Month*, November 1979, pp. 365-367.

O'Brien, Robert Y., "The Church as the Cohesive Element in Religious Education," *The Living Light*, Vol. 12, no. 2, 1977, pp. 256-259.

O'Keefe, Joan, "Sharing the Light of Faith in the Parish," *The Living Light*, Vol. 16, no. 2, Summer 1979, pp. 244-250.

Place, Michael D., "Reflections of a Moral Theologian," *The Living Light*, Vol. 16, no. 2, pp. 179-190.

Position Papers and Recommendations from the Symposium on the Parish and the Educational Mission of the Church. Department of Education, United States Catholic Conference, 1978.

Potvin, Raymond H., "Research, Theory and Practice in Religious Education: A Triadic Bond," from *Catechesis: Realities and Visions*, pp. 19-26.

Power, David N., "The Mystery Which Is Worship," *The Living Light*, Vol. 16, no. 2, 1979, pp. 168-178.

Reichert, Richard, "The Religious Educator, the Parish and Polarization," *The Living Light*, Vol. 12, no. 1, Spring 1979, pp. 76-86.

Rouet, Albert, "Catechese et Liturgie: Radiographie d'un de bat Insuffisant," *La Maison-Dieu*, no. 140, 1979, pp. 7-23.

Russell, Brother Frank, S.M., "Let's Face. the Facts: High School CCD Is Dead," *The Tablet*, May 9, 1981, pp. 31, 37-38.

Ryan, Archbishop Dermot, "The Place of Memorization in Catechetics" (Statement at 1977 Synod of Bishops), *Origins*, October 27, 1977, Vol. 7, no. 19, pp. 298-299.

Sawicki, Marianne and Marthaler, Berard, L., "No Final Word," *Catechesis: Realities and Visions*, pp. 180-188.

Sharing the Light of Faith: National Catechetical Directory for Catholics of the United States. Department of Education, United States Catholic Conference, 1979.

Sharing the Light of Faith: An Official Commentary. Department of Education, United States Catholic Conference, 1981.

"The State of Catechesis in the United States" (Report of National Conference of Catholic Bishops to the Synod Secretariat), *Origins*, April 21, 1977, Vol. 6, no. 44, pp. 705-708; *Origins*, April 28, 1977, Vol. 6, no. 45, pp. 718-724.

"Teach Them." A Statement of the Catholic Bishops on Catholic Schools, May 6, 1976, United States Catholic Conference.

Thompson, Andrew D., and Stamschror, Rev. Robert P., *Where Do We Go From Here.* A Survey of United States Diocesan Statements of Goals and Objectives for Religious Education and Catechesis. Department of Education, United States Catholic Conference, 1979.

Warren, Michael, "Catechesis: An Enriching Category for Religious Education," *Religious Education*, Vol. 76, no. 2, March-April 1981, pp. 115-127.

Westerhoff, III John, "A Call to Catechesis (A Response to Charles Melchert)," *The Living Light*, Vol. 14, no. 3, Fall 1977, pp. 354-358.

Wrenn, Rev. Michael J., "Religious Education at the Crossroads," *Faith and Reason*, VI, no. 4, Winter 1980, pp. 247-316.

Wynne, Edward A., "Adolescent Alienation, The Catholic Family and Catholic School Policy," from *Catechesis: Realities and Visions*, pp. 39-53.

CHAPTER TWO

Moral Education: A Comparison of Secular and Religious Models[1]

Paul C. Vitz
New York University

Many Christians today find themselves hesitant to teach Christian values, much less to defend them enthusiastically. A great part of the problem is the implicit assumption that somehow the case for secular and anti-Christian values is especially strong—stronger than the case for Christian values. What I would like to do here is to describe briefly, and to criticize what are the two most influential theories of secular values commonly found in the American school system: the first is known as Values Clarification; the second is Kohlberg's model of the stages of moral development. The critique will make it clear that Christians have little reason indeed to defer to secular values. In the final section I will present an outline of a positive Christian and Catholic model.

Part 1: Values Clarification

The Values Clarification (VC) position on moral education is the theory of Louis E. Raths and Sidney B. Simon in collaboration with several colleagues. Their approach was first developed and promulgated in the 1960's, while its widespread use in the public school system—and in Christian schools as well—has come in the last decade.

As the VC authors point out, their position had its origin in "the thinking of John Dewey." Very generally, VC is a set of related procedures designed to engage students and teachers in the active formulation and examination of values. It does not teach a particular set of values. There is no sermonizing or moralizing. The goal is to involve students in practical experiences, making them aware of *their own* feelings, *their own* ideas, *their own* beliefs, so that the choices and decisions they make are conscious and deliberate, based on their own value systems *(Values Clarification: A Handbook of Practical Strategies for Teachers and Students*, by Sidney B. Simon, Leland W. Howe and Howard Kirschenbaum, Hart, 1978, 2nd Ed., p. 18, emphasis in the original).

As this passage indicates, the VC approach claims to be very different from the direct teaching of morals or ethics ("sermonizing"), which Simon and Raths reject as a hopelessly out-dated form of "inculcation of the adults' values upon the young" (sic). This position is out-dated, they say, because today's complex society presents to the young so many inconsistent sources of values.

Parents offer one set of shoulds and should nots. The church often suggests another. The peer group offers a third view of values. Hollywood and the popular magazines, a fourth.... The spokesman for the New Left and the counterculture an eighth; and on and on (Simon, *et al.*, p. 16).

In order to enable young people to "build their own value system" Raths focuses in his system on what is called the "valuing process." Valuing is considered to be composed of seven subprocesses, which are, in this order:

Prizing one's beliefs and behaviors
   1. prizing and cherishing
   2. publicly affirming, when appropriate
Choosing one's beliefs and behaviors
   3. choosing from alternatives
   4. choosing after consideration of consequences
   5. choosing freely

Acting on one's beliefs
   6. acting
   7. acting with a pattern, consistency and repetition
   (Simon, *et. al.*, p. 19).

Values Clarification does not aim to instill particular values; rather the goal is to help students apply the seven processes of valuing to already formed beliefs and behavior patterns, and to those still emerging. The theorists then move on to classroom exercises designed to implement the processes. The exercises, called "Strategies," represent the major contribution of the recent VC theoretical writings. Before investigating these strategies, let us explore for a moment a few of the basic assumptions underlying the entire theory.

First, like all forms of moral relativism, this process does not encourage serious rational reflection on moral issues. Instead, it begins with the irrational, emotional prizing of whatever the student already happens to have as values or goals—and the secondary purpose of evaluation of consequences is overshadowed by this initial prizing, and by the emphasis on self-acceptance, rather than on the needs of others or of society.

Now, although the psychological and, one should add, educational assumptions of the VC theorists are rarely presented, and to my knowledge never explicitly defended, they are essential to the approach. Because of the neglect of any systematic treatment of these topics, it is difficult to disentangle the authors' assumptions from many of their normative statements, and from ambiguously worded claims. Nevertheless, certain basic assumptions about human nature and education are easily identifiable. At the centers of Values Clarification—as at the center of almost all secular humanist positions—is a certain concept of the self, one with a major emphasis on self-expression and self-realization.

This humanist position holds that the self is intrinsically entirely good, that corruption comes only from outside—from one's parents, and from society. This theory of human nature has dominated much of American psychotherapy, and most popular psychology and educational theory, through the ideals of self-expression and self-actualization. From Rogerian Therapy to Transactional Analysis to open classrooms and Values Clarification, "selfist" therapists and educators have sought to promote mental health and happiness through the magic door of "self-expression." Develop unconditional trust, remove inhibitions, support moral relativism, let each do his own thing, and all will be well.

Despite the popularity of humanistic self-theory, most serious psychologists have been consistently critical of this position, and recent criticisms have been especially strong. First, there is substantial objective evidence that man is not intrinsically all that good. Instead, human nature comes with a significant natural component of selfishness and aggressiveness. Evidence for this is now widely accepted by social scientists in many different disciplines, whether or not they use the term "original sin": they reject the assumption of our total innate goodness.

It is not just scientific evidence and theoretical reflection that discredit the "total intrinsic goodness" assumption. The violent, nihilistic and sadistic expression of aggression which has become commonplace in our society, including the classroom, has served to make the same point about human nature—with perhaps greater effectiveness, since it is obvious to all. The demise of our supposedly neurotic inhibitions in the classroom has not brought a great increase in student learning, happiness or mental health: if anything, the opposite seems to have occurred. In short, the assumption about the basic psychological nature of the self which stands at the heart of the Values Clarification theory is now recognized to be false, and this weakness alone, the absence of a concept of evil or sin, is enough to disqualify it as a serious candidate for a theory of moral education (e.g., see Vitz, *Psychology as Religion: The Cult of Self-Worship*).

Rational Critique

It is not merely that Values Clarification is based on seriously mistaken psychological assumptions: it is riddled with logical confusions and internal inconsistencies, as well.

The actual moral position of Raths, Simon, *et al.*, is generally personal relativism: What is good and bad is so only for a given person. And some of the time their position is anti-nomian: Values don't actually exist—there are only things which a person likes or dislikes. In both cases, it follows that blaming and praising others—and even oneself—are to be avoided. Now the relativist and anti-nomian positions involve Values Clarification in a number of very basic contradictions. These contradictions, combined with other weaknesses, completely undermine the coherence and credibility of the system.

An initial, basic contradiction is that, in spite of the relativity of all values, the theorists clearly believe that Values Clarification is good; that is, that students *should* engage in their VC program, they *should* prize this program for the clarification of values, etc. Raths, *et al.*, attack values inculcation by teachers—and yet they urge teachers to inculcate the value of clarifying values by using their system. Indeed when they argue for *their* system they begin moralizing and sermonizing like anyone else. They criticize values inculcation by others as "selling," "pushing," "forcing one's own pet values" on children at the price of reason and free inquiry. But when it comes to the value of *their* position, somehow relativism has conveniently disappeared.

Probably the major contradiction in Values Clarification derives from the anti-value or anti-nomian assumption found in the system. This position ends up—oddly but perhaps predictably enough—in authoritarianism. This outcome is beautifully identified by the Christian philosopher Nicholas Wolterstorff whose analysis I will follow here.[2] When Raths, *et al.*, bring up the question of whether the child should be allowed to choose anything he wishes, they answer: No. Parents and teachers have the right to set some "choices" as off-limits. But they do not have this right because those choices are wrong! It is simply that certain choices would be *intolerable* or unpleasant to the parent or teacher. "Thus" —as Wolterstörff so acutely puts it—"does antinomianism turn into arbitrary authority." The only basis for the forbidding of a particular choice is that the teacher or parent finds that choice personally offensive or inconvenient. This most disturbing "logic" is instructively demonstrated by the VC theorists themselves in the following remarkable example:

> Teacher: So some of you think it is best to be honest on tests, is that right? (Some heads nod affirmatively.) And some of you think dishonesty is all right? (A few hesitant and slight nods.) And I guess some of you are not certain. (Heads nod.) Well, are there any other choices or is it just a matter of dishonesty vs. honesty?
>
> Sam: You could be honest some of the time and dishonest some of the time.
>
> Teacher: Does that sound like a possible choice, class? (Heads nod.) Any other alternatives to choose from?
>
> Tracy: You could be honest in some situations and not in others. For example, I am not honest when a friend asks about an ugly dress, at least sometimes. (Laughter.)
>
> Teacher: Is that a possible choice, class? (Heads nod again.) Any other alternatives?
>
> Sam: It seems to me that you have to be all one way or all the other.
>
> Teacher: Just a minute, Sam. As usual we are first looking for the alternatives that there are in the issue. Later we'll try to look at any choice that you may have selected. Any other alternatives, class? (No response.) Well, then, let's list the four possibilities that we have on the board and I'm going to ask that each of you do two things for yourself: 1. see if you

can identify any other choices in this issue of honesty and dishonesty, and 2. consider the consequences of each alternative and see which ones you prefer. Later, we will have buzz groups in which you can discuss this and see if you are able to make a choice and if you want to make your choice part of your actual behavior. That is something you must do for yourself.

Ginger: (She is well named!) Does that mean that we can decide for ourselves whether we should be honest on tests here?

Teacher: No, that means that you can decide on the value. I personally value honesty; and although you may choose to be dishonest, I shall insist that we be honest on our tests here. In other areas of your life, you may have more freedom to be dishonest, but one can't do anything any time, and in this class I shall expect honesty on tests.

Ginger: But then how can we decide for ourselves? Aren't you telling us what to value?

Sam: Sure, you're telling us what we should do and believe in.

Teacher: Not exactly, I don't mean to tell you what you should value. That's up to you. But I do mean that in this class, not elsewhere necessarily, you have to be honest on tests or suffer certain consequences. I merely mean that I cannot give tests without the rule of honesty. All of you who choose dishonesty as a value may not practice it here, that's all I'm saying. Further questions anyone?
(Raths, *et al.*, pp. 114-115)

From this flabbergasting example, we might suggest as analogies: "You are not to be a racist, or drug addict, or thief, in my class, but elsewhere—that is up to you!" Or: "You are not to assault me in my class. I insist that you be peaceful here, but whether you choose to do this in other classes, or to other teachers—that is up to you!"

The great irony is that one of the acknowledged major problems within American education today is discipline. Attacks on teachers and students in the school are now so common as to represent a significant cause of low teacher morale. Now the VC approach to morality has nothing in it which can counter this problem; indeed the VC theorists provide a nice rationale to encourage student-initiated violence. After all, if the student prizes, and chooses—and (why not?) *cherishes*—his capacity for physical violence, there is no basis other than the arbitrary authority of the teacher to prevent the student's expressing it. The question is: is the teacher strong enough to *enforce* his authority—for the whole issue boils down of course to a matter of power.

Now it is unlikely that much of the recent violence in classrooms is in fact due to students' responding to their Values Clarification sessions—but it is likely that *teachers* have been affected by the program. It is to be expected that a common response to the VC sessions—in which thousands of teachers have participated—must be that teachers have no, absolutely no, confidence in their legitimate moral authority with respect to their students. This cannot but undermine the teachers' self-confidence and basic respect for their profession. And we all know that students are very good at sensing any lack of assurance in their teachers, and move quickly to exploit it.

A Critique of Procedures and Strategies

A major part of Values Clarification is the set of classroom exercises which exemplify the system in action. These procedures or "strategies" are the vehicles for the discussion and clarification of values within the framework of the VC system. They have provided a primary reason for the popularity of the approach, and even those Christian educators aware of the anti-Christian philosophy of Values Clarification have often used the exercises, under the assumption that they at least are neutral tools with which to approach the topic of moral education.

Now almost all the strategies focus on the child's self: what does he like, want, feel; what would he *vote for?*

This kind of "opinion poll" questioning has become a cultural reflex for Americans today. And of course this very approach to moral issues promotes moral relativism. In contrast, an absolute system of knowledge and values would focus attention on the objective truth, on the external reality which the student must attempt to come to know. Thus, a Christian teacher might ask, not "What do you love?" or "What do you value?" but "What are those things which are to be loved?" and "What are those things of highest value?" The emphasis would be not on *opinion*, but on truth. In short, this would be a very different approach indeed from that of VC—and it demonstrates that the VC strategies are *far* from neutral.

Furthermore, the content itself of many VC questions betrays the preoccupations and values of the permissive secular humanist. Here are examples of the questions suggested for use with all ages: these issues are to be discussed and voted on in the class.

> Would you favor a law to limit families to two children?
> Think we ought to legalize "pot" (marijuana)?
> Approve of abortion?
> Think the job of parenting should be shared by all adults?
> Would not mind having class with no textbooks?
> (Simon, *et al.*, pp. 44-48)

Here are questions typical of those recommended for secondary students and adults:

> Approve of premarital sex for boys?
> Approve of premarital sex for girls?
> Think sex education should be taught in the schools?
> Think sex education instruction in the schools should include techniques (!) for lovemaking, contraception?
> Would approve of a marriage between homosexuals being sanctioned by priest, minister or rabbi?
> Would approve of a young couple trying out marriage by living together for six months before actually getting married?

> Would encourage legal abortion for an unwed daughter?
> Have spoken with homosexuals about their life style?
> Would take your children to religious services even if they did not want to go?
> Would approve of contract marriages in which the marriage would come up for renewal every few years?
> Would be upset if your daughter were living with a man who had no intentions of marriage? If your son were living with a woman, etc.?
> Would be upset if organized religion disappeared?
> Think the government should help support daycare centers for working mothers?
> Think that parents should be subsidized to pick any school they want for their children?
> Think we should legalize mercy killings?
>
> (Simon, *et al.*, pp. 49-53)

It is not just that their questions reflect—inculcate, push—the liberal secular humanistic agenda; even the very wording of their questions suggests, *solicits*, a particular response—one in line with their philosophy. For example, when they want a positive answer they start a question with "approve" or "would approve"; when it is a negative answer that they want, they use a different approach. For example, in "Would be upset if organized religion disappeared?" the word "upset" suggests something negative and inappropriate. And of course, they don't ask the balancing questions, such as "Would be upset if public schools disappeared?" (How about "Would be upset if Values Clarification disappeared?"!) Two other questions make the same sort of point in another way. Consider the item: "Think the government should *help support* daycare centers for working mothers?" Here, the answer is clearly supposed to be Yes; whereas in "Think that parents should be *subsidized* to pick any school they want for their children?" the bias is unmistakably—by the very choice of words—toward No. That is, in the first question tax money "helps support," but in the second, tax money is called a "subsidy." Why not ask the second question this way: "Think the government should restrict children to the public school rather than to the school the student freely chooses?" Such a wording invites quite a different way of viewing the issue—and quite a different answer. In short, the questions provided by the VC manuals demonstrate considerable bias, in particular, support for the growth of state-controlled humanistic education, and an attack on any threat to this monopoly.

One could easily draw up a list of different questions, different wordings for a discussion in which religious values were taken seriously. In the VC list, there are no questions about prayer, about the religious life or about the religious virtues. Why not questions like: Do you pray often? Should you pray more? What are the advantages of chastity? What does love mean? Is love the same as sex? as feeling good? I think the point should be clear....

But the very procedures of Values Clarification have value-laden consequences. The concern with increasing the number of alternative positions on a given issue reinforces in a procedural way the idea that values are all relative. Since each of the different values is likely to be embodied by one of the student's peers, it is very hard psychologically for the student to maintain a firm belief in absolute values without experiencing painful peer rejection, and without having to reject his classmates in return. It is very hard even for adults to reject a belief or behavior without also appearing to reject the person who holds the belief or exhibits that behavior (hard, in a word, to hate sins and not sinners).

Perhaps the most destructive procedure in this system, however, is the way in which the public discussion of intimate family life undermines the authority of the father and mother. These exercises focus on classroom discussion of everything from family rules about money, chores and dating, to parental values and sanctions concerning masturbation, homosexuality and premarital sex. This procedure easily alienates children and parents. It also violates the right to privacy of the student and his parents. It appears that much of the angry and increasingly successful rejection of Values Clarification programs in public schools has come from parents' deep dismay over this issue—the public discussion of the private concerns of family life.

A Christian Response

Since Values Clarification as a theory of moral education is based on a concept of the complete innate goodness of the self, on the relativity or nonexistence of values, and on procedures which undermine parental authority, it is obviously unacceptable for Christians, in the light of basic Christian teachings. In its claim that all opinions or values are of equal weight, it denies the existence of God-given values—and implicitly the existence of God as well. It denies the basic Christian tenet of our intrinsic tendency to sin and of our obligation to struggle with evil. And it has no true notion of love, certainly no Christian idea of love; the duty to love—like all duties—is rejected.

But on the grounds of common sense and natural reason as well, the Values Clarification program and all those like it should be rejected. The internal contradictions and incoherence of the system provide—in this writer's experience—one of the shallowest and intellectually most confused systems of thought which he has ever come across. In spite of the theorists' explicit claims to be free of "pushing" any values, the VC system is a thinly disguised vehicle for hustling both moral relativism and permissive, liberal, secular humanism—while claiming objectivity. Certainly Christian values—clearly and honestly announced as such—represent a refreshing comparison. Furthermore, Christians should reflect on the fact that Christian values (many of which are common to all the world's great religions) have stood the test of time, throughout many different cultures and historical periods. And finally: Christians should have perfect confidence in the values given to us and endorsed by our Lord and our Church.

Part 2: Kohlberg's Theory

Starting in the late 1950's Lawrence Kohlberg of Harvard University began developing a theory of the stages of moral growth which has become widely influential in educational and child psychology, and in the American public school system. Kohlberg's ideas have also had great impact on Christian moral education, especially in Catholic schools. For example, I have even been informed that in some parishes Kohlberg is required reading for the young in preparation for Confirmation. Apparently with the decline of pre-Vatican II (or traditional) approaches to moral education, Kohlberg's position has been actively welcomed as a replacement: it has filled a theoretical vacuum. As a result, Kohlbergian moral education theory has acquired an informal "nihil obstat" within the world of Catholic education. As I did in my previous article on Values Clarification, I will here take a hard—a very hard—look at this approach to moral education.

General Character

Kohlberg's theory is based on the philosophy of John Dewey and the earlier work of Swiss psychologist Jean Piaget, but in many of its concepts, methods and applications Kohlberg has gone substantially beyond Dewey and Piaget to produce his own model of how moral reasoning develops in the child. The basic research strategy has been to present moral dilemmas to children and young people and then to observe the reasons given for why one course of action should be followed rather than another. Kohlberg claims to have observed that the patterns of reasoning which people use are quite distinct and few in number; specifically, he has proposed that there are six types or patterns of moral reasoning.

Before turning to these six stages, let us note that Kohlberg is interested in the person's dominant pattern of moral reasoning: he is concerned with the form and process of the thought used, not with the actual moral outcome, the actual decision made. Thus, two people may disagree about what is to be done but use the same kind of reasoning, or they may come to the same conclusion but for very different reasons. Like so many modern thinkers he is concerned with structure and changes in structure (process) but not in content.

Kohlberg comes to far-reaching conclusions about the set of patterns of moral thought he claims to have observed. What he believes to have discovered is that when a person is studied over a number of years the evidence shows that he goes through a developmental series in these moral patterns. Each pattern of moral reasoning in the sequence represents a qualitatively distinct "stage" in the person's life. Further, Kohlberg claims that the sequence of stages is the same for all people, although some may never get to the higher stages. Since he proposes that there are six stages this means that everyone develops morally by starting at stage 1 and over time proceeds moving on up in order from 2 to 6, unless growth stops at an intermediate stage. According to Kohlberg nobody ever skips a stage and nobody ever regresses to an earlier stage. He does, however, allow for people to show a mixture of two adjacent stages, that is, a person can be in a transition between two stages. Very briefly, the stages are:

Stage One:	Punishment-Obedience Orientation
Stage Two:	Instrumental-Exchange Orientation
Stage Three:	Good Boy-Nice Girl Orientation
Stage Four:	System-Maintaining (or Law and Order) Orientation
Stage Five:	Social-Contract Orientation
Stage Six:	Universal Ethical-Principles Orientation

In more detail they are defined by Kohlberg as follows:

I. PRECONVENTIONAL LEVEL

At this level the child is responsive to cultural rules and labels of good and bad, right or wrong, but interprets these labels in terms of either the physical or the hedonistic consequences of action (punishment, reward, exchange or favors) or in terms of the physical power of those who enunciate the rules and labels. The level comprises the following two stages:

Stage 1 *punishment and obedience orientation* The physical consequences of action determine its goodness or badness regardless of the human meaning or value of these consequences. Avoidance of punishment and unquestioning deference to power are valued in their own right, not in terms of respect for an underlying moral order supported by punishment and authority (the latter being Stage 4).

Stage 2 *instrumental relativist orientation* Right action consists of that which instrumentally satisfies one's own needs and occasionally the needs of others. Human relations are viewed in terms similar to those of the market place. Elements of fairness, of reciprocity, and equal sharing are present, but they are always interpreted in a physical pragmatic way. Reciprocity is a matter of "you scratch my back and I'll scratch yours," not of loyalty, gratitude, or justice.

II. CONVENTIONAL LEVEL

At this level, maintaining the expectations of the individual's family, group, or nation is perceived as valuable in its own right, regardless of immediate and obvious consequences. The attitude is one not only of *conformity* to personal expectations and social order, but of loyalty to it, of actively *maintaining*, supporting, and justifying the order and of identifying with the persons or group involved in it. This level comprises the following two stages:

Stage 3 *interpersonal concordance or "good boy-nice girl" orientation* Good behavior is that which pleases or helps others and is approved by them. There is much conformity to stereotypical images of what is majority or "natural" behavior. Behavior is frequently judged by intention: "he means well" becomes important for the first time. One earns approval by being "nice."

Stage 4 *"law and order" orientation* There is orientation toward authority, fixed rules, and the maintenance of the social order. Right behavior consists of doing one's duty, showing respect for authority, and maintaining the given social order for its own sake.

III. POST-CONVENTIONAL, AUTONOMOUS, OR PRINCIPLED LEVEL

At this level there is a clear effort to define moral values and principles that have validity and application apart from the authority of the groups of persons holding these principles and apart from the individual's own identification with these groups. This level again has two stages:

Stage 5 *social-contract legalistic orientation* Generally, this stage has utilitarian overtones. Right action tends to be defined in terms of general individual rights and in terms of standards that have been critically examined and agreed upon by the whole society. There is a clear awareness of the relativism of personal values and opinions and a corresponding emphasis on procedural rules for reaching consensus. Aside from what is constitutionally and democratically agreed upon, the right is a matter of personal "values" and "opinion." The result is an emphasis upon the "legal point of view," but with an emphasis upon the possibility of changing law in terms of rational consideration of social utility (rather than freezing it in terms of Stage 4 "law and order"). Outside the legal realm, free agreement and contract is the binding element of obligation. This is the "official" morality of the United States government and constitution.

Stage 6 *universal ethical-principle orientation* Right is defined by the decision of conscience in accord with self-chosen ethical principles appealing to logical comprehensiveness, universality, and consistency. These principles are abstract and ethical (the Golden Rule, the categorical imperative); they are not concrete moral rules like the Ten Commandments. At heart, these are universal principles of justice, of the reciprocity and equality of human rights and of respect for the dignity of human beings as individual persons.

Lawrence Kohlberg, "Stages of Moral Development as a Basis for Moral Education," pp. 86-87 in Beck, *et al.*, *Moral Education: Interdisciplinary Approaches* (Toronto: University of Toronto Press, 1971).

The Empirical Critique

The first question we must ask—before moving to rational contradictions and ideological bias—is whether the extensive research using and investigating Kohlberg's theory has generally supported the theory's main assumptions: first the existence of the six stages, and second the tendency over time for individuals to move from a lower to a higher stage and not to regress to a lower, earlier stage. This is not the place to go into a detailed summary of the very extensive research literature; instead I will present the main conclusions of a thorough review of this issue published in 1974. More recent evidence bearing on this issue will also be included.

The psychologists Kurtines and Greif in their review (*Psychological Bulletin, 81,* 1974, 453-470) of the evidence bearing on Kohlberg's theory make the following summary conclusions after discussing the first fifteen years of relevant studies.

1. The six stages as described are arbitrary and unclear.
2. The scale which consists of a set of moral dilemmas (Moral Judgment Scale) has not been standardized: i.e., the actual dilemmas used in

the scale have not been fixed in number or in kind; the scoring procedure has been frequently revised, changed, and is often ambiguous. This has resulted in rather frequent use of scoring categories like "ambiguous," "transitional," etc. In one large study, 46% of the responses could not be placed in any stage. The scale's revisions make earlier experiments no longer interpretable. Moreover, the scoring manual has not been published and is available only by writing to Kohlberg.
3. As of 1974 there were no published data on the reliability of the scale, and evidence suggests that people's scores fluctuate greatly even over short periods of time.
4. There is no evidence that scores on the Moral Development Scale can predict any kind of moral action. (Indeed one study reports that activist students at Berkeley were predominantly either at Stage 6 or at Stage 2. These two very different levels of reasoning led to identical behavior.) In other words there is no evidence that Kohlberg's stages have any practical bearing on conduct. There is in particular no evidence suggesting that the final three stages have any predictive significance. The authors suggest that a scale that divided subjects into two categories such as mature-immature would account for whatever predictive significance Kohlberg's scale of stages has demonstrated.
5. Examination of types of evidence offered in support of the idea that the sequence of stages is invariable revealed no clear support for this position, and the cross-cultural data on early development provide no support for qualitative differences between stages or for their fixed order. Elizabeth Leonie Simpson, in a review (*Human Development*, 17, 1974, 81-106) addressed just to the issue of cross-cultural evidence

for Kohlberg's stages, concludes: "...The definitions of stages and the assumptions underlying them, including the view that the scheme is universally applicable, are ethnocentric and culturally biased." This is perhaps too broad an accusation, for there is *some* cross-cultural support—but the ideological character of Kohlberg's system would certainly support Simpson's general point. Kurtines and Greif note studies which provide considerable counter-evidence to Kohlberg's assumption that moral development is basically a form of natural intellectual maturation. These studies show that moral judgment can be affected by social influence, such as modeling by a child of an adult figure. In summary Kurtines and Greif write:

> We can only conclude that the value of the model remains to be demonstrated.

Although Kurtines and Greif have not gone completely unchallenged by Kohlbergians, the great majority of their criticisms have been accepted by many psychologists and even in crucial ways by Kohlberg himself. Kohlberg has acknowledged that the scale of moral development has never been standardized and has constantly been changed as a result of new problems with the earlier dilemmas; he also acknowledges that the scale reliability and validity are not really known and that the scale is still only available through his laboratory where it is constantly under revision. He is now trying to remedy these weaknesses and to make a standard scale generally available. Kohlberg does, however, defend the empirical existence of the different stages and their developmental order. He claims that recent evidence to some degree supports his sequence of stages. Of course he now admits that stage regression may recur:

> Pointing out that none of his longitudinal subjects had achieved stage six by 1976, Kohlberg lamented at a recent symposium: "Perhaps all the sixth-stage

persons of the 1960's had been wiped out, perhaps they had regressed, or maybe it was all my imagination in the first place" (Quoted in *Psychology Today*, February 1979, p. 57).

(The last clause of this quotation is perhaps the most interesting one—and Kohlberg's "humility" may be altogether appropriate. In any case, the idea has dawned on him!) He later conceded—after a recent longitudinal study in America and Turkey in which Stage 6 did not occur at all—that maybe the problem was not *regression*, but that Stage 6 did not exist:

> This result (that is, the failure to find a Stage 6) indicated that my sixth stage was mainly a theoretical construction suggested by the writings of "elite" figures like Martin Luther King, not an empirically confirmed developmental construct.... We now think the safest interpretation would be to view the construct of a sixth stage as representing an elaboration of the B (or advanced) substage of Stage 5 (*New Directions for Child Development*, 2, 1978, p. 86).

In spite of Kohlberg's attempt to defend the very existence of his stages, many psychologists are dubious indeed. Professor Robert Hogan (John Hopkins), an especially lucid critic of Kohlberg, quite flatly states that there is *no* evidence that Kohlberg's stages exist. Of course different patterns of moral reasoning or explanation exist, but the evidence for stage sequence, especially with respect to the higher stages, does not exist, according to Hogan. Hogan bases his position partly on the fact, still true as of late 1980, that Kohlberg's scale for measuring stages has not met the necessary standards of reliability, validity, etc., to justify *any* conclusions about stage existence, much less the order of supposed natural development. Hogan also bases his criticism on evidence from his own research that strongly suggests, for example, that the difference between Stage 5 and Stage 6 (as between what Kohlberg now calls 5A and 5B) individuals is a difference in personality type. To claim that it is a difference in the *level* of moral maturity is, Hogan argues, simply a scientifically unacceptable expression of Kohlberg's own political beliefs. (See below.)

In conclusion, the empirical support for Kohlberg's model is very tenuous at best, and although the issue is still an active one, at present the system is beleaguered, and quite possibly it is already fading. One prominent researcher, Joseph Adelson of the University of Michigan, commented, "I suspect the system (of Kohlberg) is beginning to fall apart." Kohlberg himself describes his model as a "leaky boat" requiring much patching and which may sink.

We now examine other types of criticism, which have been steadily increasing in recent years.

The Rational Critique

The central philosophic difficulty in Kohlberg's model is his assumption that moral development can be characterized as a development in morally neutral rational competence without regard to actual moral decisions, without regard to moral content. Now, Kohlberg emphatically rejects moral relativism, and he believes his approach avoids the errors of relativism:

> The cognitive-developmental or progressive view (Kohlberg's view) claims that, at heart, morality represents a set of *rational principles* of *judgment and decision* valid for every culture.... Our research into the stages in the development of moral reasoning, then, provides the key to a new approach to moral education as the stimulation of children's moral judgment to the next stage of development (emphasis Kohlberg; from *The Humanist*, Nov.-Dec., 1972, p. 14).

When psychologists such as Piaget talk about stages of intellectual development, however, they not only speak of the development of greater cognitive flexibility and differentiation, but they also show that the higher level leads to correct or more nearly correct answers.

They show how the child has a better understanding of an agreed upon external truth, for example, a truth of logic or mathematics, or a truth about perceptual reality. But with morality the idea of reality testing—of being right—is rejected by Kohlberg, since he claims that there is no such possibility. This preoccupation with structure and its development without an absolute standard leads, ultimately, as will be shown, to the very moral relativism Kohlberg supposedly rejects. As in my previous article, I would like to acknowledge my debt to Wolterstörff (*Education for Responsible Action*, Grand Rapids, Michigan: Eerdmans, 1980) whose analysis I will often follow in my remarks below.

Why and how does a person move from a lower to a higher stage? The Kohlbergian rationale goes something like this. A person at a lower stage discovers that moral questions become too complex and too conflicting in terms of the concepts which he is currently using. The pressure for cognitive integration and equilibrium leads him to formulate a new set of principles in order to handle moral issues more adequately. At each new and higher stage the person is cognitively more differentiated (complex) and more cognitively integrated in a way that allows him to resolve the cognitive dissonance which facilitates this growth. This, according to Kohlberg, is role-taking. (Role-taking for Kohlberg means the "tendency to react to others as like the self, and to react to the self's behavior from the other's point of view.") Kohlberg posits that the impulse to take the role of others is natural, and that this leads to a natural concern for fairness and justice. It is this role-taking in increasingly more varied and complex moral situations that is therefore central to moral education.

Kohlberg's general strategy requires that his concept of cognitive adequacy be value-neutral. He is not, then, claiming that the role-taking impulse and the pattern of reasoning it sets in motion are "good." These are simply natural facts, like any other forms of natural growth and development. In spite of this claim of value-neutrality,

Kohlberg is, however, frequently ambivalent on the matter. He says, for example: "At every stage, children perceive basic values like the value of human life, and are able to empathize and take the roles of other persons...." This is not entirely a descriptive comment, for it suggests that people at all stages recognize life as good, and that it is in fact good. His tendency to slide—without noticing—back and forth from neutral descriptions of morality to the implicit valuing of such things as life and role-taking abilities, to the value of development *per se*, and finally to the valuing of the justice principle, is a serious logical confusion in Kohlberg's system. The fact is that Kohlberg's system is profoundly relativistic. Let us look in some detail at certain statements of Kohlberg's—and here I follow rather closely the Wolterstorffian analysis. Kohlberg says he does not believe "that moral judgments describe the states of the world in [...] the same way as scientific judgments describe the states of the world." Instead, moral judgments and norms are ultimately to be understood as universal mental constructs which regulate social interaction. Thus, Kohlberg writes: "A higher conception of the value of love or a higher conception of moral emotion...is not directly truer than a lower conception." He goes on in a most peculiar passage to say:

> Our claim that stage 6 is a more moral code of thought than lower stages is not the claim that we can or should grade individuals as more or less moral. We argue elsewhere that there is no valid or final meaning to judging or grading persons as morally better or worse. Judgments on persons as morally good or bad or judgments of praise and blame are not justified by the existence of universal moral principles as such. At the highest stage, the principle of justice (or the principle of maximizing human welfare) prescribes an obligation to act justly (or to blame the unjust) or give us rules for meting out blame to the unjust. Although there are some rational grounds for punishment, there are no ultimately rational or moral grounds for blaming other people. From a moral point of view, the moral

worth of all persons is ultimately the same; it is equal (Kohlberg, p. 48 in Beck, *et al.*).

What has Kohlberg said? Wolterstörff struggles nobly with this confused passage by first observing that Kohlberg's basic point is that it is never right, as such, or wrong, as such, to do something. Instead, actions are only right or wrong relative to a certain principle. Relative to the justice principle, an action might be wrong. But relative to a utility principle, the same action might be right. And, Kohlberg seems to be arguing, there is no way to determine whether any principle is more right or wrong than another. It is not possible to choose an incorrect principle, as Wolterstörff concludes: "All one can do is apply correctly or incorrectly whatever principle one has chosen."

If Wolterstörff's interpretation is correct—and I, like him, can see no alternate interpretation—then Kohlberg holds a special kind of anti-nomian position. Wolterstörff suggests the name "principle-relative-antinomianism." In any case, Kohlberg considers there to be no absolute moral basis for making a moral judgment about principles of morality. This is a position he shares with Jean-Paul Sartre, R. M. Hare and others. In short, despite his frequent denials of the validity of moral relativism, he ends up there himself.

But the fact that Kohlberg's system is riddled with relativism does not keep it from being profoundly permeated with an unacknowledged ideology as well. Kohlberg's critics have long claimed that his Stage 6 (now, as we noted, jettisoned) was there all along not because of any data, but because Kohlberg liked it: he valued that level of morality most highly; he saw it not merely as the "last" but truly as the highest, the *best* of his stages.

Kohlberg defends the principle of justice behind his Stages 5A and 5B (né 6) because he claims it has the following three properties: it is *universal* in that it applies to all persons and all actions. Second, it is *prescriptive* in that it states what should or ought to be done. And third, the principle of justice is *autonomous*, for it makes no appeal to any other authority, or to what anyone else holds on moral matters.

Now if Kohlberg means only that these criteria describe the nature of a principle at the highest level of natural development, he has a problem. First, there are other possible principles besides justice which would fill the same requirements: Wolterstörff points out that the *negation* of justice meets all the same formal requirements. Evil can be just as "rationalized" as good. As for other possible principles, such as those based on utility, mercy—and above all a principle of love—these are simply ignored. On the other hand, there are times when Kohlberg seems to imply that his criteria for a principle are themselves intrinsically good. It is clear, for example, that Kohlberg believes that autonomy, i.e., independence from any authority, is a desirable quality. When he slips into this mode of expression, he has of course violated his pose of neutrality. He has taken an ideological stance.

Apparently, it is not just Kohlberg's critics who have been disturbed by his tendency to mix values with the supposed neutral processes of moral steps. Kohlberg himself—after twenty years of insisting on neutrality in moral education—has finally reversed his position:

> Although the moral stage concept is valuable for research purposes, however, it is not a sufficient guide to the moral educator, who deals with concrete morality in a school world in which value content, as well as structure, behavior as well as reasoning, must be dealt with. In this context, the educator must be a socializer, teaching value content and behavior, not merely a Socratic facilitator of development. In becoming a socializer and advocate, the teacher moves into "indoctrination," a step that I originally believed to be invalid both philosophically and psychologically. I thought indoctrination invalid philosophically because the value content taught was culturally and personally relative, and because

> teaching value content was a violation of the child's rights. I thought indoctrination invalid psychologically because it could not lead to meaningful structural change. I no longer hold these negative views of indoctrinative moral education, and I now believe that the concepts guiding moral education must be partly indoctrinative *(The Humanist, op. cit.,* pp. 14-15).

This dramatic about-face by Kohlberg retroactively changes the meaning of his previous work a great deal—and suggests his own basic uncertainty about it. In any case, until he integrates this new position with his former work, the present critique stands. At a minimum, he would have to make explicit the particular values in his indoctrination. Be that as it may, the supposed "moral neutrality" of Kohlberg's present system can be rejected outright—and that was one of the major bases for its support. But the bias in Kohlberg's system goes still deeper.

The Ideological Critique

The most recent and powerful attacks on Kohlberg, all from secular social scientists, have focused on the positical and ideological assumptions—the doctrine—embedded in his position. The most important of these have been the critiques by Sullivan and by Hogan and Emler.[3] I will present their analysis in some detail, leaning primarily on the work of the latter two psychologists. This critique is extremely important because it is leveled not only against Kohlberg, but against social psychology as a whole, and indeed against all social science. It is part of the now rapidly growing awareness within social science that there is no neutral or objective theory, nor is such theory in principle even possible. This collapse of the implicit assumption of objectivity among social scientists has profound and encouraging implications for the use of Christian models of human nature within what has been called impartial social "science."

Hogan and Emler very generally see Kohlberg's theory as an expression of liberal ideology. Specifically, they charge it with containing four major assumptions which Kohlberg has not examined or even made explicit, assumptions of an intrinsically ideological kind.

The first assumption is that of *rationalism*. For Kohlberg, moral development is an entirely cognitive process. He is concerned only with setting up abstract moral problems or dilemmas which pit various rather abstract principles against each other. His intent is to focus reasoning on a choice between two different moral principles, in such a way that the person's criteria for the choice are revealed. The concern is with getting rational argument from the subject—argument or reasons that defend his choice. Kohlberg's position totally ignores moral action. (I might add: there is no concern at all with the will.) Equally obvious is Kohlberg's neglect of the profound emotional and interpersonal elements involved in all natural moral dilemmas. For Kohlberg, the Cartesian "I think, therefore I am" is clearly his fundamental approach to understanding the human moral situation. Kohlberg's use of highly abstract and often contrived moral dilemmas is one expression of his extreme rationalism. Apparently, Kohlberg is also now backing away from this property of his work, for he has recently spoken disparagingly of his hypothetical abstract rational examples as "science fiction" dilemmas.

Kohlberg also assumes that the natural direction of moral development supports and implies *individualism*. That is, he assumes that morality develops toward internalized moral controls in which the individual is socially and morally autonomous. Each individual is presumed to be able to ultimately discover for himself a natural morality that owes nothing to cultural or historical heritage. The belief in the isolated autonomous individual is of course a fiction, since it is itself an expression— a creature—produced by our particular contemporary secular humanist culture.

Kohlberg simply assumes, without discussion, that obedience to the self—to one's internal code—is superior to obedience to God, to a divine code. The nature of this self is not presented by Kohlberg, but he appears to assume that it is intrinsically entirely good, and that there is no problem of evil. If this is so, then the criticism of this psychological position made in the case of Values Clarification holds with equal force for Kohlberg.

The assumption of individualism, as Hogan and Emler note, is smuggled into Kohlberg's theory by the use of moral issues which involve primarily individualistic values, such as property, civil rights, the value of human life, individual conscience. Thus his examples implicitly assert the moral conclusion that "an individual's rights to life, and control over his or her own affairs are the paramount values in life."

Another basic assumption of Kohlberg is that of *liberalism*. Hogan and Emler identify Stage 6, with its concern with the concept of justice, as an expression of Kohlberg's personal philosophy. They identify the moral philosophies of Kant, Hare and especially John Rawls as influencing Kohlberg here. It seems inappropriate for present purposes to go into a detailed treatment of liberal moral philosophy. This we can say: whatever moral philosophy one adopts, liberal or otherwise, one must acknowledge it. One cannot just imply that one's own theory is the pure scientific statement of how human nature spontaneously develops when it grows to its highest stage—as verified by objective evidence.

A further criticism of Kohlberg's theory is that it is *androcentric*, that is, that it expresses a "characteristically masculine view of morality." Carol Gilligan, a colleague of Kohlberg, has made this point rather well, although I would suggest that the issue is that Kohlberg's system is at least as anti-*Christian* as it is anti-*feminine*. Gilligan points out that the initial 1958 study, which is still the core of empirical support, was run exclusively on young male subjects—from which Kohlberg then generalized to all humanity! Gilligan also claims that the preoccupation with male values—I would say really *modernist* values—such as rationalism, individualism, and liberalism—is responsible for the fact that adult females in comparison to males are found (according to Kohlberg) disproportionately in Stage 3. Males tended to be "more morally advanced," and located at Stage 4. (Stage 3 is "good boy-nice girl," or conventional morality; Stage 4 is "system-maintaining morality," e.g., law and order.) Kohlberg has responded to this criticism by deciding he made a mistake in how he scored Stage 4! He has subsequently claimed that many males who had been scored at Stage 4 were really giving answers at Stage 2. That such an error could have been made for so many years strikingly underlines the ideological biases present in the scoring system, and further reduces confidence in it.

Gilligan succinctly summarizes the quite different approach to moral problems taken by women. Consider the well-known Kohlberg "science fiction" dilemma of Heinz. Heinz must steal a drug from a village druggist since it costs much more than he can pay—or else he must let his wife die.

> Here in the light of its probable outcome—his wife dead, or Heinz in jail, brutalized by the violence of the experience and his life compromised by a record of felony—the dilemma itself changes. Its resolution has less to do with the relative weights of life and property in an abstract moral conception than with the collision it has produced between two lives, formerly conjoined but now in opposition, where the continuation of one life can now occur only at the expense of the other. Given this construction, it becomes clear why consideration (for women) revolves around the issue of sacrifice and why guilt becomes the inevitable concomitant of either resolution *(Harvard Educational Review,* 47, 1977, p. 512).

She continues:

> The proclivity of women to reconstruct hypothetical dilemmas in terms of the real, to request or supply

> the information missing about the nature of the people and the places where they live, shifts their judgment away from the hierarchical ordering of principles and the formal procedures of decision-making that are critical for scoring at Kohlberg's highest stages. Given the constraints of Kohlberg's system and the biases in his research sample, this different orientation can only be construed as a failure in development. While several of the women in the research sample clearly articulated what Kohlberg regarded as a postconventional metaethical position, none of them were considered by Kohlberg to be principled in their normative moral judgments. Instead, the women's judgments pointed toward an identification of the violence inherent in the dilemma itself which was seen to compromise the justice of any of its possible resolutions. This construction of the dilemma led the women to recast the moral judgment from a consideration of the good to a choice between evils *(ibid.).*

She quite correctly proposes that in giving exclusive moral weight to the principle of justice, Kohlberg underestimates the moral worth of other principles, especially mercy. Hogan and Emler describe this—as does Gilligan—by citing Shakespeare:

> Thus, the female virtue of mercy becomes a Stage 3 conception. But, as Portia reminds Shylock, mercy qualifies justice..."though justice be thy plea, consider this, that in the course of justice, none of us should see salvation. We do pray for mercy."

Gilligan sees Kohlberg's absence of concern for interpersonal and emotional issues in moral problems as androcentrism. A Christian would simply point out that the principle of *love* as a synthesis of mercy and justice is in fact a *higher* principle than justice alone.

One final ideological bias in Kohlberg, not mentioned by Hogan and Emler, is his *atheism*. This assumption lies behind Kohlberg's favoring of individual autonomy and explains his placing answers giving a religious rationale at Stage 4. As mentioned, he assumes, among other things, that any reasoning based on the acceptance of authority, human or divine, derives from rules, not from principles. Christian love, however, *is* a principle in the Kohlbergian sense.

It is important to keep in mind that when Kohlberg's system is introduced into schools, Christian parents are made to think they are at a lower moral level than the Stage 6 secular humanist goal of the program. Since the parents aren't in a position to see through Kohlberg, such Christians are "put down" very heavily—and most unjustly—by educationists who present the Kohlberg system as the latest thing in impartial science.

I will conclude with an example from Kohlberg's description of his scoring system which makes very clear this kind of anti-religious prejudice in his theory. The respondent, a boy named Richard, was asked for his moral reaction to mercy killing. He replied:

> I don't know. In one way, it's murder; it's not a right or a privilege of man to decide who shall live and who should die. God put life into everybody on earth and you're taking away something from that person that came directly from God, and you're destroying something that is very sacred; it's in a way part of God and it's almost destroying a part of God when you kill a person. There's something of God in everyone.

Kohlberg comments:

> Here Richard clearly displays a Stage 4 concept of life as sacred in terms of its place in a categorical moral or religious order. The value of human life is universal, it is true for all humans. It is still, however, dependent on something else, upon respect for God and God's authority; it is not an autonomous human value. Presumably if God told Richard to murder, as God commanded Abraham to murder Isaac, he would do so ("The Child as Moral Philosopher," in *Readings in Developmental Psychology Today*, Cem Books, 1970, pp. 111-112).

Kohlberg simply assumes that the culturally determined principle of "an autonomous human value" is higher than one based on obedience to God! Thus does his scoring system express—and expose—his ideology.

Furthermore, it is not at all clear how this last answer is a standard Stage 4 answer. That is, it is not obviously directed at system-maintaining, or law-and-order. Apparently, a belief in the sacredness of life and obedience to God is to Kohlberg the same thing as Archie Bunker's defense of lower-middle-class American law and order.

Although Kohlberg's theory is of interest to those doing research on moral development, his theory's empirical, rational and ideological weaknesses—not to mention its incompatibility with Catholic teaching—are so great that one is hard put to find any good reason for its present widespread use in Christian moral education. In any case, Kohlberg himself is an avowed humanist, and appears to have been surprised by the favor with which he has been viewed by Christian—primarily Catholic—educators. So far as I can discover, Christian enthusiasm for Kohlberg's theory just seems to be one more pathetic example of Christians slouching toward secularism—in this case, a secularism that even the secularists are abandoning.

Part 3: Toward a Christian Model of Moral Development

In this section I will propose in rough outline form a Catholic Christian theory of moral development. I am not attempting to present a thoroughly worked out theory or model, but only to sketch out some basic principles and concepts which any theory would, I believe, have to include.[4] One major purpose of such a proposal is to attempt to move from the critical stance exemplified in the two previous articles in this series, to a positive statement. If believing Christians are to have any lasting impact, they must begin to move from the critique of modernism to the development of concrete positive alternatives. I do not wish to downplay the importance of a thorough critical analysis of the crisis brought on by the growth of modern secular thought in our society and within Christianity itself. I have done a good deal of this myself. But criticism is only the first stage in a successful counter-movement. To stay too long in this critical stage is to risk getting bogged down in a negative mentality—a mentality which can reinforce passivity, blind reactionary rejection, and occasionally verge on despair. Christians must develop positive programs for de-secularizing society and for re-introducing Christ into the emerging post-modern world. After all, we are in a kind of horse race with the secularists, and to win a race you need a horse (or horses), not just good pre-race information on the strengths and weaknesses of the other fellows' horses. We should keep in mind that the old saying is quite true: the best defense is a good offense—and it is much more fun besides!

Before beginning, let us review briefly some of the major weaknesses in the secular humanist approaches to moral education—these weaknesses can indeed be called the dilemmas of moral education. First, these approaches ignore man's natural tendency to evil: to selfishness, to exploitation, to aggression and to cruelty. This lack of any concept of evil is a major flaw in the humanist theories in general—and it is a particularly devastating one when such theories are explicitly applied to moral knowledge and growth.

Second, the absence of any concept of a clear objective basis for the moral life inevitably leads into relativism—which is exactly where all these approaches end up. Now moral relativism may be temporarily expedient in a pluralistic society, but as a theory of moral education it must fail: it can justify *nothing*—including education, and including itself. More accurately perhaps: it can justify *anything:* every conceivable crime, every sin has in recent years had its justification made: murder (political expression), suicide (death with dignity), adultery and incest (life-enhancing sexual freedom)—not to mention abortion (pro-choice), etc.

Third, a central concept in secular morality is the "autonomous individual" or self. Now it is becoming increasingly clear that this supposedly autonomous individual is a figment of the secular liberal imagination. In point of fact these autonomous creatures are—despite their illusions of autonomy—strongly controlled by the economical and philosophical needs of a consumer society and the political needs of the secular state.

Fourth, the secular moral theories typically go from what *is* to what *should be.* That is, because some kind of behavior exists they typically assume that it therefore has some intrinsic moral legitimacy.

This fallacy is common to both humanistic and biologically-based attempts to arrive at a moral theory. It is, however, simply a fundamental error in logic to assume that "is" can justify "should." Such an assumption also typically ends up in a kind of relativism as well, since *any* behavior which exists can thus be justified.

A final major flaw in the secular approaches to morality has been their ancient pattern of failing to reach any kind of agreement about the nature of what is moral. Secular thought seems intrinsically unable to come to any agreement or reasonable concensus about moral principles. Indeed, philosophers and social scientists appear wedded to the need for novelty, intellectual innovation and to the desire to perpetually question all things. Since theories of morality, like all theories in the world of philosophy and social science, are constantly changing, they are incapable of serving as systems for teaching children morality. Values Clarification and Kohlberg's model are two cases in point.

This weakness has been clearly identified in a written intervention at the 1977 Synod of the National Conference of Bishops. Here it was observed:

...disciplines like psychology, sociology, pedagogy, and anthropology can make a significant contribution to catechesis.

However, catechists must realize that these sciences are constantly changing, as new discoveries are made and old theories discarded. Furthermore, they do not supply the doctrinal and moral content of catechesis, nor are they the source of ultimate values. It is also important not to suppose that only those considered "normal" by the criteria of the human sciences can receive and respond to God's gifts. *Pope John Paul II: Catechist*, Chicago: Franciscan Herald, 1980, p. 192, [Revs. R. J. Levis and M. J. Wrenn, Editors]).

Related to the perpetually changing content of secular moral theory has been the fascination by catechists with new teaching techniques. No doubt much of the appeal of Values Clarification and of Kohlberg's model has been the novel techniques associated with each. Again the Church, here Pius XII, has spoken directly to the problem:

No educational method, be it based on some particular tradition or developed by modern educational science, can give perfect and lasting results if it disagrees with Christian principles, or scorns their values, or fails to use true Christian means, including supernatural ones. Christianity is not only able to complete any other pedagogical method, but possesses its own safe method to lead souls to the highest perfection, as largely demonstrated by its saints *(Pope John Paul II, Catechist,* [Revs. Levis and Wrenn, p. 123]).

And finally John Paul II in *Catechesi tradendae* has realistically questioned teaching methods "dictated by more or less subjective theories or prejudices stamped with a certain ideology" *(ibid.,* p. 122). The Holy Father also writes in Article #58 that: "A technique is of value only to the extent that it serves the Faith that is to be transmitted and learned; otherwise it is of no value" *(ibid.,* p. 122). Both comments apply most obviously to those Christians who have become enamored of the systems just discussed here.

We turn now to an outline of a possible Christian model of moral education.

The Model

The foundation assumption (axiom) of revelation. A Catholic Christian theory of moral education must start with the assumption of God's revelation of the moral life to mankind as expressed in Scripture and as maintained and elaborated by the Church. This assumption solves the four dilemmas discussed above. The moral understanding of the human condition revealed in Scripture clearly acknowledges man's capacity for evil (and explains that it is located in our will); it provides an objective basis for morality, gives man free will to choose the moral life—and allows him to become truly independent of the surrounding social pressures ("Be ye not conformed to the world..."). Finally, it provides a clear basis for knowing what should be done. In short, the assumption of revelation is (in the technical sense of the word) "parsimonious" and powerful: that is, the acceptance of this one assumption solves many otherwise unsolvable or most complex difficulties. Furthermore, in accepting revelation, one is accepting a moral tradition which has functioned effectively in the lives of millions, in a great variety of cultures, over a two thousand year period. This is not a morality concocted by some philosopher or psychologist only to be forgotten or "updated" in a few years.

The principle of love. The central moral revelation and the first principle of the model is the revelation of God's love for us, and of our obligation to love Him and to love each other. Let us recall Christ's formulation of our fundamental obligations as His followers:

> You shall love the Lord your God with all your heart, and with all your soul, and with all your strength, and with all your mind; you shall love your neighbor as yourself (Luke 10:27).

It is important to underline in these commandments that our first obligation is to love God, is to direct ourselves to the transcendent, to the vertical dimension of reality. The second and horizontal requirement is that we love our neighbor as ourself. This principle of love requires that we show not only mercy and forgiveness to others, but also fairness or justice in our relationships to them. "The Gospels know no emotion worthily designated as love, whether applied to God in heaven or to His incarnate Son, which is unconditioned by righteousness and justice."[5] Thus, the Christian principle of love is a synthesis or integration of mercy and justice—and constitutes a higher principle than Kohlberg's principle of justice alone. This principle of Christian love is also universal in its applicability to all people, and it is prescriptive in that it is something which we "should" do. Christian love is also autonomous, with respect to any purely human authority, or to any other principle. (Certainly obedience to the authority of the autonomous self—as in Kohlberg and other humanists—is obedience to a most human and socially determined authority.) These characteristics make it clear that Kohlberg's requirements for a basic moral principle (as discussed in my previous article) can be met even more strongly by Christian love than by humanistic justice alone.

Emphasis on the will. However important knowledge, reason and cognitive skills may be to the moral life, they are not, within a Christian framework, to be considered central. The great emphasis in any Christian theory must be on aligning one's will with God's. It is no accident that relatively few of the many great loving Christians, from the Apostles to St. Francis of Assisi to Mother Teresa, have been intellectuals or scholars. Intellectual acuteness and love can occur together, as with St. Thomas Aquinas, but even then the priority is on love. (Remember that Aquinas said that next to the revelation he received of divine truth and love, all his writings seemed like "straw.") Indeed, we are called to be as little children, not as philosophers or wise men. In today's highly intellectualized world it is most crucial to remember this. The Christian way is not the Greek way of Gnosis; Christian morality is not dependent on having a high I.Q. Jesus was not primarily helping His disciples to acquire knowledge, but to achieve an understanding of what they were to do: whom they were to love, whom they were to obey and follow. And we are to love, obey, follow not our own will—our own "choices"—but God's will: "Not my will, but thine."

This concern with the will should take three forms: the will to pray and worship—the heart; the will to understand basic Christian doctrine—the head; and the will to loving action—the hands.

Christ as Model.[6] In addition to the love of God and the alignment of our will with His, as *principles* of the moral life, Christians are given a very clear role *model* as well: Jesus. Thus, the fundamental psychological concept of role-modeling—of identification—is central to Christian moral development. He is "the way, the truth and the life;" we are to imitate Christ and to "grow into the fullness of the stature of Christ." Thus, a psychological principle considered important for moral development by secular psychologists is deeply embedded in the Christian moral life—namely, taking the role of the other. The second commandment's wording makes this clear: we are to love others *as ourselves.*

Good vs. Evil—and a proposed Moral Acquisition Device. The Christian tradition has always maintained that evil exists and that everyone is, in part, evil: no one is righteous before God. Further, the introduction of evil into our life is through the contamination not of our body but of our will.

Not only are we all "fallen"—in part, evil—but we *know* it. Now of course some, a very few, deny that they know it, but I would like to propose that the starting point of moral development is the period during which children develop a natural understanding, however primitive, of good and evil, and of the difference between them. Thus, I would propose that a more accurate beginning of moral life—in contrast to both Kohlberg's and Piaget's "Stage 1"—involves an innate (that is, naturally and spontaneously emerging) moral sense. It develops through the operation of what I will call a Moral Acquisition Device (MAD).[7] This device is, I think, operating in the child by the age of two or three—at least based upon my own observations of a number of children. My thinking here is then opposed to the recent assumption in psychology that the basic concept of morality does not occur in children, and that all that exists is something brought to bear on children, from the outside, with rewards and punishments. I reject the Stage 1 of Kohlberg which is indistinguishable from models of simple animal learning based on positive and negative reinforcement, and it implicitly denies that there is anything intrinsically *human* about a child's moral life. (These learning models have never fared well when applied to distinctively human activities such as language.) I believe a Christian model of morality would challenge such behaviorist assumptions as applied to the moral nature of the child.

What is the nature of this Moral Acquisition Device? I suggest that the child is naturally aware of the emotional state of love—normally of his love for his mother and his father, and the state of being loved by them. This experience is not primarily an externally manipulated "reinforcement." Instead, it is above all an internal state or experience, involving not only the child's awareness of the mother, but also an awareness of the internal cues of love, e.g., feelings of warmth, comfort, trust, happiness. In addition, it seems reasonable to suppose that the child naturally knows that this state is "good." Indeed love is surely the domain of our experience to which the term "good" first applies. The second factor in the innate moral acquisition is the child's experiences of pain, anger, jealousy and even hate. Again, there are internal conditions or cues which identify these for the child in ways which I believe are far more important than the externally perceived events that bring them about. These latter experiences serve as the initial basis for the category "bad." A final factor in the Moral Acquisition Device is the child's awareness that these two fundamental states conflict: that they are opposites. Very early, a child understands the desirability of goodness and the disturbing character of badness, and the basic conflict between them: the two are mutually exclusive, as experiences.

Children also very early, by two or three, understand the meaning of obedience and disobedience, and understand that in general disobedience is bad. The previous Moral Acquisition Device contains the logic for how they arrive at this knowledge. For example, if the parent asks the child to do something which the child knows to be good, and the child disobeys, then he knows that his disobedience is also bad. If in general the parent asks the child to do good things (which is normally the case), then the child easily learns that disobedience—that is, disobeying a loving authority—is bad. It is essential that any theory of moral education and development deal with the issue of obedience and disobedience, that is, obedience to properly constituted authority. American social scientists either totally ignore this issue, on the basis of their political philosophy, or come down heavily in favor of a total personal autonomy. This American hostility to obedience to anything except self (and self-defined interests) has become so extreme as to be pathological.

This emphasis on the child's innate capacity for an understanding of the basic moral issues of good vs. evil is not to be interpreted as a claim that all morality is equally innate. It is simply a claim that the structure of basic or core morality has to do with the conflict between good and evil as related to people—to our experiences of people—and ultimately with loving and hating (and being loved and hated). It is also to state that the great moral issue is a battle over the control of the will— obedience vs. disobedience—and thus of the basis for our choices between good and bad. The first and great moral issue, even for children, is: are they going to be good, or bad? And, superimposed on this fundamental choice: are they going to obey the good, as represented by a loving parent, or are they going to disobey, and do "as they please"? It is worth noting that, unlike the categories and concepts of Values Clarification and Kohlberg, the present model stresses the categories of the actual situation in which children and their parents find themselves: good/bad, obedience/disobedience are at the very heart of children's early experience of the moral life. These are no contrived moral dilemmas.

I should perhaps clarify one point. The present model is essentially an innate phenomenological model. That is, the emphasis on the innate origin of basic moral conflicts puts the model in the theoretical tradition not only of the ethologists and sociobiologists but of Chomsky's conceptualization of language as well. Indeed the term "Moral Acquisition Device" is modeled on his "Language Acquisition Device"—a term at the heart of his theory of the innate basis of language. But the notion that the child must experience certain emotional states also puts this model in the tradition of the phenomenologists, e.g., Husserl, Scheler—and Pope John Paul II. Finally, the concept that the child is aware of an opposition between good and bad—love and hate—and is *free to choose* between them places this model to some degree in the Existentialist tradition as well.

The centrality of prayer. As noted earlier, it is not of trivial significance to our moral life that the *first* commandment is to love God, and the *second* commandment to love neighbor and self. I am arguing, therefore, that a program of Christian moral development should always begin with a focus on our moral relationship to God before addressing the issue of our moral relationship to other people. Specifically, this means that Christian moral development is not possible without prayer and participation in worship—that is specifically the sacraments. This point is extremely important, for although Christianity has great respect for the moral law, its primary message is to love God and to do His will, and we cannot do this unless we seek to love and know Him: no set of laws can replace our direct experience of God and the receiving of His grace. (It is our prayer life, our spiritual life, that is the major basis of the experience of God and grace.) The secular humanists like to think that Christians obey an "arbitrary external authority." No doubt some do. But the core of the Christian moral and spiritual life is a living relationship with God. It is crucial to note here that those Christians actively practicing the expression of love to others have universally acknowledged the centrality of prayer in their lives. For example, Father Bruce Ritter in New York City who has founded homes for runaway teenagers in the Times Square area requires three hours of prayer daily from those who volunteer to help him. Prayer is also a major activity in Chuck Colson's prison reform movement, and in the communities founded by Mother Teresa of Calcutta.

Without God's grace, law becomes rigid and formalistic—and vulnerable to being manipulated in the service of our own self-righteousness. This is in no way to suggest that we should deny the law, or that we are above it; instead, the point is that unless God is alive in us, we cannot express the spirit of the law, which is love. Loving God and loving our neighbor as ourself—the Christian principle of love—is necessary for the true fulfilling of the law.

The will re-emphasized. A further emphasis on the will is in terms of the second commandment. Since "faith without works is dead," Christian moral development must involve Christian moral *action.* It is not enough just to pray, or to know the law—or to sit around and talk about how we are to love others—without there being an expression of this love in *works.* (In fact, we do not even really understand what we do not practice.)

> We beg and exhort you in the Lord Jesus that, even as you learned from us how to conduct yourselves in a way pleasing to God—which you are doing—so you must learn to make still greater progress (1 Thessalonians 4:1).

Therefore, any model of Christian moral development must include not just the knowledge and experience of prayer—which is the essential starting point—but it must also include exercises in loving actions. Or as Wolterstörff puts it in a somewhat different context: "Christian education must have as its goal responsible action." A prerequisite for reliably helping children to reach such a goal is a theory of Christian education. (Wolterstörff's new book should provide a pioneering contribution to such a theory for he develops a Christian framework of the philosophical and psychological factors involved in inculcating tendencies to action.)[8]

Outline of a Christian Moral Development Program: Age levels 1, 2 and 3. I will not be speaking here of qualitatively distinct stages of Christian moral development. (Whether such stages exist is at present an unanswered question, but one open to empirical investigation. There is a long tradition of theory and evidence supporting the position that Christian spiritual growth —as in the life of prayer, exemplified by St. Teresa, St. John of the Cross, etc.—does develop in three major stages. Whether a program for children integrating the life of prayer and knowledge with good works would result in distinct stages is, however, not known, as far as I can gather.)

By the term "level," I mean an age level with its associated natural degree of intellectual development, plus whatever emotional preoccupations typify children of the age in question. These natural stages of intellectual and emotional development are very loosely characterized here—and there may be a good case for alternative understandings of the three ages selected. I also assume that the child's natural level of development, whatever it is, is subject to radical qualitative transformation through the effects of grace. Let us never forget that children can become saints.

Level 1: Ages 5 to 7. The first commandment. This age is the time for the learning of prayers by rote memory, and for the general development of the habit of prayer. It is a much neglected commonplace that the early years of life are the best for the learning of things "by heart" and for the acquisition of basic habits. It is not necessary that all the prayers be fully comprehended by the intellect. The contemporary over-emphasis on rational, abstract understanding is another form of the rationalist assumption.

Here I completely agree with section 176.e of the National Catechetical Directory "Sharing the Light of Faith" which puts it as follows:

> While catechesis cannot be limited to the repetition of formulas and it is essential that formulas and facts pertaining to faith be understood, memorization has nevertheless had a special place in the handing-on of the faith throughout the ages and should continue to have such a place today, especially in catechetical programs for the young. It should be adapted to the level and ability of the child and introduced in a gradual manner, through a process which, begun early, continues gradually, flexibly and never slavishly (p. 102).

There are many things in life that we learn—and must learn—long before we fully comprehend them: for example, the simple laws of multiplication and division. (I have been informed by my mathematician friends that I still do not fully "comprehend" these laws.) And who "understands" Mother Goose rhymes, which children have loved—and found meaningful—for centuries? It is also well worth noting that children get great pleasure from memorization: it is an accomplishment which they can take with them and demonstrate wherever they go. And to know certain things by heart is never to be alone. For example, recently a friend of mine, a wobbly atheist, was out in the woods chopping firewood. He was at some distance from his house, and he was alone. He accidently slammed the ax into his leg, cutting himself quite badly. As he painfully climbed the hill to his house—aware that he might bleed to death before he got to the top—he found himself reciting the Lord's Prayer. There are many times when children are alone, lost, vulnerable—when their reason is no match for their anxieties and fears, and when we are not there to protect or comfort them: what can we give to them more precious than prayers?

Here it is relevant to bring in an important topic which so far has had little impact on education— especially religious education. Over the last 20 years or so extensive research on the brain has shown that the two halves of the cerebral cortex are specialized for different modes of thought and knowledge. Very roughly the left side of the brain which controls speech and the right side of the body is specialized for verbal, analytical, and rational tasks. The other half, the right side of the brain, is specialized for spatial, non-verbal, e.g., bodily movement, and more intuitive types of knowledge. Those educators who restrict learning to cognitive, rational types of knowledge which can be clearly verbalized, e.g., Kohlberg, are failing to allow for the qualitatively different but equally important right brain type of knowledge. Still more important are those activities like prayer which involve both words and images and which serve to *integrate* both types of knowing. For example, the rosary involves words, images and bodily movements such as crossing one's self as well as holding the crucifix and the beads—very integrative. Many forms of popular Catholic piety which have been summarily dismissed from Catholic education can probably be given a powerful new educational rationale by the brain hemisphere research. (For references see: J. E. Bogen, "Some educational aspects of hemispheric specialization." *U.C.L.A. Educator, 17,* 1975, pp. 24-32; B. Edwards, *Drawing on the right side of the brain,* Los Angeles: Tarcher, 1979; S. J. Dimond and J. G. Beaumont (eds.) *Hemisphere function in the human brain,* New York: Wiley, 1974; R. W. Sperry, "Hemisphere disconnection and unity in conscious awareness," *American Psychologist, 23,* 1968, pp. 723-733.)

But the fundamental issue is that prayer is the beginning of spiritual life; it is the way in which children learn to open themselves to God, and hence it is the beginning of the moral life, and of the life of worship. Such prayers then also allow the child to participate in worship. The encouragement of regular private prayer also belongs in the initial emphasis on the first commandment. Basic prayers are also, of course, an introduction to theology, to the knowledge of Christian moral principles.

The second commandment. The second commandment component at this level might be exercises in which the child is encouraged to demonstrate love of his "neighbor." In contrast to programs which talk about abstract principles and people who live ten thousand miles away, a Christian program should, I believe, first focus on the child's family and immediate friends. The exercises or procedures to facilitate this have not been developed, but they would entail the expression of love, caring and forgiveness within the family and for close friends. Close, supportive talks—one to one, adult with child—both at home and at school fit in here. (I would welcome further suggestions as to specific "exercises.") Prayer for each other belongs in this category. In particular, prayer in small groups can be an especially strong religious experience for children, for example, praying for those who are ill or suffering in each other's families. Recently I observed a group of about twenty first-graders being introduced (far too briefly) to the concept of prayer. In the group was a little girl whom I knew was being raised by her grandmother after the recent death of her mother and father. She asked whether it was possible to pray for someone who was dead. She was greatly relieved and moved to hear that you could. She would have been even more moved, I'm sure, if by good fortune the priest (who did not know the girl's background) had responded by encouraging the children to pray then and there for the child's mother and father—and for her and her grandmother, too. Praying for people is the beginning of love for them.

Level 2: Ages 11 to 13. At this age the child first develops a modest level of adult reasoning—and, of course, puberty brings up sexuality as a central preoccupation. First commandment: a) The maintenance and elucidation of the prayers already learned. b) First retreat: one day. c) Brief introduction to Christian meditation. d) Discussion of ways to maintain a schedule of daily prayer. Second commandment: This emphasis would involve expression of "good works" in the students' community. The focus would move out from the family into the immediate community. Both commandments: a) This is a good time to introduce the rational basis for moral theology. Children here are ready for an introduction to argument. Let them have fun honing their minds while defending the basic tenets of their Faith. Let them, for example, find the flaws in moral relativism. b) Now, if not earlier, they can also be introduced to the lives of the saints and other such reading. c) This is also an age at which it would be appropriate to introduce concepts of Christian sexual morality—by that I mean not just "love" (by itself, that could quickly present problems!), but Christian virtues such as chastity, courage and prudence, and the general strengthening of the will.

Level 3: Ages 16 to 19. At this age, the personal problem of an adult identity and the common preoccupation with "romance" and challenge are the central themes around which to build moral development. Here loving God can be gone into in considerable depth. I would suggest the following exercises or projects. First commandment: a) A more extensive introduction to the practice of Christian meditation. b) A retreat of at least two or three days. c) The spiritual rationale of the fast, and its practice. Second commandment: The expression of love in the form of good works in the larger community. Giving of time, e.g., one day every two weeks—a kind of time tithe. This service could be given in many settings. For example, hospitals, schools, old people's homes, working with a religious community, working in prison missions. (On a more limited, local scale such service could also be done earlier: for example, offering to baby-sit with the children of a sick mother.) Both commandments: a)

Reading Scripture. b) Reading the lives of the saints and other great Christians (e.g., Bonhoeffer, Martin Luther King). c) Reading great religious literature, especially poetry. d) Possibly, active participation in evangelization.

This is also the time to broaden the idea of morality so as to include the moral life as it relates to marriage, adult sexuality, and to general moral concepts such as the virtues (see P. T. Geach, Joseph Pieper).

The preceding model is obviously quite sketchy, and there are, no doubt, different emphases possible within both the Catholic and Protestant tradition. The point, however, has been to show how *very* different a Christian theory of moral education and development would be from a secular humanist approach. It has one other purpose. At present Christians appear to have had one of two responses to secular theories of moral education. Either they ignore the issue and leave the field to the secularists by sheer default, or they water down their Faith by uncritically joining secularism. It is time for the rich heritage of Christian moral thought to be used to challenge the present disastrous situation.

FOOTNOTES

1. This paper is based in part on a series of articles appearing in the *New Oxford Review*, 1981. Aspects of this article are also developed more extensively in *Psychology as Religion: The Cult of Self-Worship*, Grand Rapids, Eerdmans, 1977.

2. See *Educating for Responsible Action*, by Nicholas Wolterstorff, Grand Rapids, Eerdmans, 1980.

3. I highly recommend the Hogan and Emler article, which is especially strong: "The Biases in Contemporary Social Psychology," *Social Research*, 45, 1978, 478-534.

4. Since I plan to develop this work further, any suggestions or criticisms from readers about the issue of Christian moral education are most welcome. My address is: Department of Psychology, New York University, 6 Washington Place, New York, N.Y. 10003.

5. Carl F. H. Henry, *Christian Personal Ethics*, Eerdmans, 1957, p. 414.

6. In the practical sense the present model is *Christocentric*—another feature in common with the emphasis in *Catechesi tradendae*.

7. This terminology was suggested by the psychologist Clinton W. McLemore.

8. Nicholas Wolterstörff, *Education for Responsible Action*, Eerdmans, 1980.

CHAPTER THREE

Catechizing the Poor

Sister Michelle McKeon, S.C.
Saints Peter and Paul Parish
South Bronx

Before we begin I would like to express my gratitude for the invitation to share some practical experience with you today. I consider this opportunity a great privilege and also a first—the first time that I have ever attended a symposium—let alone spoken at one.

In preparing for today's topic on "Catechizing the Poor," I was reminded of another first in my life: Some thirteen years ago, as a very young Sister, I began teaching at Saints Peter and Paul School in the South Bronx and was as eager to teach the third grade religion class as I am to share some thoughts with you today.

In my enthusiasm to teach the children about the Holy Father all the necessary points were covered, and I thought that the message had finally entered into their heads. Just to make sure I asked: "Now, boys and girls, can anyone tell the class who is Pope Paul VI?" One bright light named Carlos, whom I will never forget, raised his hand and said: "Pope Paul VI is the *son* of Pope Paul V." Needless to say that lesson went straight out the window and I learned very quickly to alter my teaching technique.

I do hope that the following reflections on Catechizing the Poor make more of an impression on you than that religion class made on the children. At the end I will be happy to try to answer any of your questions.

During the past year the media and movie critics bombarded us with critiques about the movie "Fort

Apache—The Bronx," which depicts the Hispanic community as a Sodom and Gomorrah. The picture was filmed at the police station across from our parish school.

I have been told that our convent, school and Cathedral-like church are even pictured in the movie. This is very sad because this "R" rated movie portrays only a miserable side of life. Since Hollywood wants sensationalism and money, the film makers missed an essential part of the South Bronx. They missed the *good* people who make up the Church—our Church—who share our Faith as Catholics.

The combination of the spiritual heritage of the immigrant Hispanics, together with family catechetical instruction and the practice of their Faith, carry on the Church's tradition. Our faithful Catholic families are never written up in the newspapers. They will not win Hollywood's Academy Awards, nor could they define the term *catechesis;* but they are dedicated to Christ, to family life, to worship, and to parish life, just as we are.

This afternoon I wish to present some practical aspects of this dedication by developing four significant signs: the first is the sign of *confianza* (a Spanish word meaning the building up of trust and confidence); this will be followed by the sign of *contradiction,* the sign of *vitality,* and the sign of *hope.* All these signs mark the ministry of catechizing the poor so that they may know Christ and the fullness of His message.

By way of a preface, much of the fruit of this insight is the result of sharing prayer and a traditional religious life-style with eight other Sisters who range in age from 35 to 75. Our average of thirteen years of teaching experience and parish involvement in Saints Peter and Paul has certainly motivated us to foster confianza among those to whom we minister.

The poor who live in the inner city, predominantly Blacks and Hispanics, are economically referred to as the minorities. However, we who teach them rather refer to them spiritually as the majority because of their simple faith—a faith that has always sustained the Church.

It is this faith which is the bedrock for developing confianza. Moreover, it is this simple faith which accepts the concrete manifestations of confianza—that of affirmation and sensitivity which should permeate our catechetical instruction. These qualities are not only necessary in "handing on our teaching" among the poor but are fundamental and crucial to any effective catechesis.

Pope John Paul II during his visit to the South Bronx both affirmed and was sensitive to our people in the midst of the deprivation that surrounded them. As the Holy Father traveled within our parish boundaries our parents and children not only saw a visible sign of Christ's love for them but were encouraged by the Pope, our principal catechist, to look to Christ.

This affirmation must be constantly demonstrated by those involved in the ministry of teaching our Faith. In a home mission area it is the groundwork, the basic springboard to bring others to know Christ and become faithful members of the Church.

My Sisters in Community all believe in and practice this affirmation in many ways: from sharing a Spanish meal in a tenement apartment, counseling members of families after school, visiting the home of troubled students, praying with parishioners in our local hospital and grieving with a family at the death of a grandparent. In short, performing our corporal works of mercy certainly speaks volumes to our people and lays the foundation for confidence and trust. They come to know Christ because they experience Christlike people on a first-hand basis.

Our Hispanic poor are turned off by functionaries; those who perform instead of identifying with them and their needs, their culture and their spiritual heritage and values. Hispanic faith is manifested strongly in the value attached to the providence of God, to prayer, to familiarity with God and with the saints, to the acceptance of suffering and the cross, and devotion to our Lady in the family.

Upon entering an Hispanic home one immediately notices the shrine altar with its varied statues and candles. *"Yo soy muy católica."* "I am very Catholic," is a usual response. Furthermore, a blessing is always bestowed on anyone who enters or leaves the humble apartment.

We must capitalize on these Hispanic values and be sensitive to their cultural Catholicism which is influenced by fatalism, by spiritism, and by a practice of *promesas,* in which our Hispanic women *promise* to wear a homemade religious habit for a designated period of time as a sacrifice for a special intention. We must also be aware of the vigorous attempts at evangelization by the storefront Pentecostal churches who afford the people a sense of identity and community. Their appealing street corner ministers emphasize conversion from sin as well as the means of salvation, and preach a puritanical lifestyle to their followers.

Sensitivity also calls us to an awareness that the Church and school offer a spiritual and safe oasis, an ordered, comfortable Christ-centered place—a second home which counteracts the media, the street and some immoral family situations.

We must also be sensitive to the fact that our children are often street-wise due to the evils of crime, drug and alcohol addiction, to sexuality and to peer pressure, to independence due to working mothers or single parents and to the consequences of the lack of a true father figure.

Because of the instability of home life some of our children come to school or religion classes and express some hostility or aggressive behavior. This action prompts one to ask them: "Would Jesus have acted like that?" This question usually calms them down. Recently, however, José responded: "But Jesus' mother did not bring home her boyfriends."

Sensitivity runs the spectrum of various family lifestyles—from children who talk about their father's wife or my sister's mother to a child who said last week:

"Sister, if I act crazy in class, be patient with me. My father moved out of the house last night. Can we say an Our Father for him when we say our prayers today?"

Due to our society today these examples are not just representative or unique to so-called minority groups. Middle and upper class family structures also fall victim to similar pressures. However, one major difference can be seen in the approach taken to remedy or deal with the situation. Inner-city children are not sophisticated and are basically upfront about a problem. Our type children exhibit a docility and an openness to seek support. They literally entrust their lives to us for direction. This in turn becomes an awesome responsibility for the catechist.

It is not my intention to portray life in the South Bronx as a catechetical "Utopia." There are days that are riddled with frustration. Frustration comes after graduation when a great number decide to take a vacation from Church due to their feeling of independence. Follow-ups are needed as well as patience during this time of a faith crisis. Because of the foundation given to them and prayers offered for them, many do return to Church. Frustration is exemplified by a young man in our minor seminary who is constantly ridiculed by members of his family, all of whom are away from the Church. How do you try to answer his question? "Sister, how can I really be happy in heaven if probably no one in my family will be there?"

When Mother Teresa of Calcutta opened her convent in a neighboring parish, she spoke about the greatest evils that plague our families—that of despair and apathy. "Let us look straight into our families for love begins at home." If there is no stable home, the affirmation and sensitivity of the catechist create a surrogate home and deepen the bond of trust and confidence.

Now let us turn to the signs of contradiction which permeate catechesis in our South Bronx mission land. There is a phenomenon that occurs. The early immigrants who first settled in New York—the Italians, the

Poles, the Irish and the Germans—all brought their Faith and the practice of it and handed down all these aspects to their offspring.

On the contrary, due to systematic catechetical instruction, our first and second generation Hispanic children are instrumental in concretizing the practice of the faith of their parents.

For example, due to the shortage of priests in Puerto Rico, Mass is not celebrated every Sunday in all the country villages. Thus weekly attendance at Sunday Mass has not been part of the native cultural Catholicism of the people from the campos.

Our adults are actually brought to this practice and obligation through their children. This indirect instruction is also reinforced by making every effort to greet the parents after each Mass with the hope of building up the community within the Church.

Many years ago when it was necessary to defend the financial support of our school, we said quite frankly: "We would not have a vibrant parish without our school." This is precisely because our children share what they receive and in fact become junior catechists to their parents.

Our sacramental programs, passion and scriptural plays, days of recollection all become avenues for parental involvement and enhance our catechetical spectrum. Together with definite doctrinal lessons these activities deepen knowledge, build up confidence and often return parents to the sacramental life of the Church.

Recently at a First Penance celebration a mother witnessed her daughter's peaceful smile after leaving the reconciliation room: "My daughter, Jessica, looks so peaceful and happy." Needless to say the mother also sought that sacramental peace.

There are many non-Catholics who attend our school and social activities. All such children must attend religion classes and become actively involved in them. We find that many of our Baptist children are very vocal and contribute to prayers and scriptural discussions. This year our non-Catholic parents were invited to attend information classes about our Catholic Faith. This past Easter seven of our school children were baptized. Catechesis certainly sets the stage for evangelization and in this way builds up Christ's Church among the poor.

Talking to someone on the corner or walking into an apartment project with a veil on your head easily marks you as a sign of contradiction to the value system of the neighborhood. This witness carries many messages even though the results are very often undetected. Catechesis is taught through this witness and through the stability of our presence with the children.

Whenever our children are asked what is the most important subject in our school, unanimously the answer will be: "Religion." The older grades will inevitably add: "building our character." If catechesis does not build character, it lacks a core ingredient.

I wish to share true examples of character formation and moral development to illustrate the importance of fundamental catechesis.

In discussing the sixth commandment with a rather "old" sixth grade class, Harry stood up defiantly as if I were contradicting a family code. The macho spirit which was definitely implanted in him from his father and uncles certainly deemed me old-fashioned and the Church's laws unrealistic. Harry announced generally to the class that it was perfectly all right for Puerto Rican boys to have sex with their girlfriends.

One year later Harry rang the convent bell and stood there very remorseful, nervous and guilty. He asked to be forgiven because, through his own experience, he now realized that he was wrong. The point of the story is that the seeds of moral development were planted and the conscience formation was taking shape despite other influences of home and environment.

Just a month ago one of the Sisters woke me at 5:30 a.m. to say that Randy was downstairs for confession. At that hour, I mumbled something about not being ordained, and then found my way to the parlor. After being rejected by his family two years ago and moving a thousand miles away, Randy had just returned to the Bronx. He had come to apologize because our last encounter had been rather unpleasant due to the fact that he had announced his homosexuality and his condemnation of the Church's position. Randy said: "I miss going to Mass regularly and being associated with my second home at Saints Peter and Paul." He then presented a poster which I could barely read at that hour. It read: "Our lives are shaped by those who love us and by those who fail to love us."

These examples emphasize the practical level of how our youth need moral development and conscience formation as well as doctrinal knowledge. They need this teaching to fall back upon when they make their mistakes, and they need it to shape the future of their lives.

The sign of vitality concretely takes shape from the daily instruction which embodies our rich deposit of faith. Due to the transiency rate of our area, we make a consistent effort each year to repeat our systematic approach to doctrine all across the grades and in so doing supplement our textbook series.

A new trend in educational circles is "Back to Basics." However, we have maintained this approach even in the midst of the swinging catechetical pendulum of the early 70's. As a consequence our children have been quite knowledgeable and dogmatically literate because of their receptivity and our reinforcement.

Children express their faith by fully participating in weekly class Masses. One can witness the marked distinction that occurs in a transfer student from public school. Within a three-month period our new students take up the spirit of worship and volunteer willingly to read, or sing, or serve.

To foster their own prayer life the children are directed in selecting themes and choosing appropriate slides for audiovisual prayer services. They eagerly volunteer to lead their friends in a class meditation. Their spontaneous prayers reflect how close the Lord is to them.

In a classroom scene it is most rewarding to enter a fifth grade class and see children easily locate scriptural passages, or enjoy filmstrips that emphasize the life of Christ and make Gospel accounts more real to them.

A competitive spirit even prompts some to devise challenging games and matching columns on scriptural quotes or on the lives of the saints or on the feast days of the Church.

During Holy Week our imaginations got the best of us and the sixth graders creatively interviewed Gospel characters as part of the "Jerusalem Eyewitness News Team." Statements like: "How did you feel, Peter, after you denied Jesus?"; or to Mary Magdalene: "You are quite a faithful friend, Mary. You did not run away from Jesus." These activities not only identify children with the events of Jesus' life but also reinforce their understanding of Salvation History which textbooks sometimes portray ineffectively.

Activities such as role-playing the miracles and parables, discussing Bible history, or comparing other religions assure that religion is not just a subject but rather something alive and personal—not second nature but part of their very nature, part of their lasting memory. These activities give them a chance to verbalize their Faith.

The language barrier of our children at times limits their conceptual development. Our Hispanic children need a working vocabulary. The apostolic exhortation emphasized that memorization among our youth is a real need. Definitions of Grace, Trinity, Incarnation, and Magisterium are known by our inner city children and the revelation of these terms is ongoing.

If it is in someone's power to grant a catechetical dream to become a reality, my dream would certainly be to have all our children memorize the same text to our common prayers.

Our children should memorize. Even our bilingual pre-school children are media-conscious and commit to memory a score of television commercials ranging from Jordache jeans to breakfast cereals.

Early exposure to faith development is most essential and may be illustrated by this true story: A young seminary professor visited our first grade class and asked: "Why did Jesus die?" Many hands were waving to eagerly answer. Lourdes responded: "Because he was a bad man!" Father was shocked and Sister blushed!

However during a subsequent lesson, Sister was teaching about obedience and stressed how Jesus was obedient to Mary and Joseph and tried to help them at home. This time Lourdes spontaneously exclaimed: "Right, Sister, Jesus was a good little kid." The message did come across.

Lastly, the sign of hope permeates our catechesis and can be seen in myriad ways. When a child is asked: "To whom do you pray?" the response usually is not just the word "God" but, I pray to our Father, or to the Spirit, or to Jesus, or to Mary, to Saint Peter or Saint Paul or to one of the other saints or to the angels or some even say, "I pray to my Grandma."

The glimmer of hope gets brighter when you see your former students become catechists and volunteer their time to assist in the sacramental program.

Our hope for the future is also expressed through some Hispanic and Anglo young women who are attracted by our religious life style and seek the answers to questions about their vocations. Days of recollection at the convent deepen their prayer life and relationship to Christ.

One interesting point is that these girls are graced with simplicity and a willingness to serve. After participating in a weekend retreat filled with quiet time, conferences and audiovisual presentations, the most meaningful part of the days for the girls was the group recitation of the Rosary which was never done before by the Irish and Italian girls but was part of the culture of the Hispanic girls.

The stability of living for many years in a parish setting produces many rays of hope. This can be seen when the fruit of years of catechetical work is evidenced by two college men, former favorite students and present close friends. Academically they have achieved. As in the case of José, he deepens his fundamental faith by attending daily Mass and by achieving A's in theology in this renowned University of Saint John's.

José's classmate, Junior, stems from a home where there have been many step-fathers. One evening on the street his third step-father said very sincerely: "Junior is very different. You people taught him religion and to respect God and obey the Church. He will be faithful to one woman."

These words are ringing loudly in my ears today because this afternoon at 4:00 p.m. it will give me great joy to read the Epistle at Junior's Nuptial Mass.

If time permitted, numerous other examples could be presented to substantiate that catechesis to our first and second generation Hispanic youth is vibrant, and that the Church is alive among our poor, and most importantly that the Church's teaching is being handed down.

Pope John Paul II realized this when he spoke directly to our people as he stood in a South Bronx lot. "I would wish that the flame of hope should not only not go out but it might increase in strength so that all of you who live in this South Bronx area may succeed in being able to live with dignity and serenity as families and as sons and daughters of God."

Before leaving New York the Holy Father stated that "every city must have a soul." It is through our people, who by their own faith have enriched our lives, that our area should not be referred to as a slum but rather as the *soul* of the South Bronx and a manifestation of the soul of the Church.

I would like to close today with a prayer written by a group of children from Saints Peter and Paul School as they reflected during the week on this Sunday's Gospel.

> Dear Blessed Mother, in this month of May we especially love you and believe in Jesus' love for us. Help us to be faithful members of His Church and to follow the words of Pope John Paul—always to look to Christ. May Jesus, your Son, always be for us the Way and the Truth and the Life. Amen.

CHAPTER FOUR

Catechesis for Adults

Sr. Theresa Catherine Shea, O.P.
Molloy College,
Rockville Centre, N.Y.

In this period of the Church, a period marked specifically by a new Pentecost, a new outpouring of the Spirit, calling for a renewal in every facet of her life, it would appear that the Church has come full circle. By that I mean her concentration has shifted from concern primarily for the proper instruction of the young (although that surely is not neglected) to a greater emphasis on the imperative that adults have an innate right to her best efforts in catechesis.

To one whose apostolate has been devoted to catechesis from that of children, through adolescence in Junior High School, to young adults in Senior High School and College, and finally, to adults in the "Teacher Training Program" of the Rockville Centre diocese, the words of our Holy Father come as a blessed affirmation of a long-cherished and strongly-felt belief that religion is for the adult. Says Pope John Paul II:

> I cannot fail to emphasize now one of the most constant concerns of the Synod Fathers, a concern imposed with vigor and urgency by present experiences throughout the world: I am referring to the central problem of the catechesis of adults. This is the principal form of catechesis, because it is addressed to persons who have the greatest responsibilities and the capacity to live the Christian message in its fullest developed form.[1]

Or to quote from the *National Catechetical Directory:*

> Since the act of faith is a free response to God's call and since maximum human freedom only comes from the self-possession of adulthood, adult catechesis is the chief form of catechesis.[2]

Therefore, just as Christ sent the Spirit on His Apostles to go and preach the good news to the first adult Christians, so Christ through His Vicar calls for a renewed apostolic mission of bringing the full message to adult Christians upon whose shoulders rests the awesome responsibility of being the leaven permeating mankind and raising it up to God the Father through Christ.

Our Holy Father in the statement quoted above pointed out that adults "have the capacity to live the Christian message in its fully developed form." What is that Christian message? At the very heart of that message is Christ, the Christ who calls each of us to a gradual growth from our initial commitment to Him in our Baptism to a fully mature Christian who with Paul can say, "I live now, not I, but Christ lives in me."[3] And again, "to me to live is Christ."[4]

When mature Christians are exposed to the full meaning of Christ in their lives, of the very personal relationship that they can enter into with Christ, a dramatic change invariably takes place. Christ no longer is a shadowy figure who became man two thousand years ago and lived His life in a culture alien to theirs: rather, He becomes a pulsating reality in the minutiae of their lives, a close companion on the way, sharing their joys and sorrows, supporting their faltering efforts at growth and lifting them above the mundane to a spiritual level where all life has meaning.

And how frequently we hear from confused, concerned Christians in a world whose very foundations seem unsteady, the haunting questions: "What is the meaning of life? Where are we headed? What is it all about?" To offer some small measure of stability, to set the feet of the questioner a little more firmly on the rock which is Christ, to place their hands in the steadying hands of Him who said: "I am the way, the truth and the life."[5] This is indeed for the catechist a most rewarding experience.

Regarding the adults who have the good fortune to enroll in classes whose end result has witnessed a radical change in their lives, how shall we measure the far-reaching effects on those whose lives they touch?

We spoke earlier of the catechesis of the young. Actually, who are their first catechists? From infancy, the values, the lifestyle, the principles of the adults surrounding them in the hallowed shelter called "home." ...All these are literally absorbed as if by osmosis by the impressionable minds and hearts of the observers. To love is to imitate. And what greater model for imitation can there be than the loved adults who themselves are steeped in the true meaning of their Christian commitment and whose lives are lived in an atmosphere permeated with Christ. Surely, these nurslings' instruction has begun long before the first official catechist has any part in their spiritual molding. As Pope John Paul so clearly states:

> Education in the Faith by parents, which should begin from the children's tenderest age, is already being given when the members of a family help each other to grow in faith through the witness of their Christian lives, a witness that is often without words but which perseveres throughout a day-to-day life lived in accordance with the Gospel.
> ....
> Family catechesis therefore precedes, accompanies and enriches all other forms of catechesis.[6]

And what can we say of the society at large within which the Christ-centered individual moves? It takes little if any imagination for one to visualize the alien milieu in which the adult Christian finds himself today. He is like an oasis in the scorching heat of sin, violence, injustice and selfishness. If ever the leavening effects of sincere Christian lives were needed, it is in today's world held in the grip of material values.

Into this maelstrom of conflicting ideologies, amidst the rise of ever new cults, and the electrifying effects of scientific ventures must be thrust the "witness of Christ," the evangelizing and sanctifying efforts of the confirmed Christian. As the Vatican II document on the apostolate of the lay people states:

> The very witness of a Christian life and good works done in a supernatural spirit are effective in drawing men to the Faith and to God; and that is why the Lord has said: "Your light must shine so brightly before men that they can see your good works and glorify your Father who is in heaven" (Mt. 15:16).[7]

It is this silent, but most effective because it is silent, witness of the transforming effect of a Christ-centered life that will have the greatest influence on a society so bankrupt spiritually that life is meaningless. The perennial questions: "What makes him different in the face of insuperable odds; how does she maintain balance in a world so off keel?" These and other queries can force the questioner to seek answers from the One who caused the question. And answers will come only if the mature adult has himself found the well-spring in the Gospel message. Like the pebble dropped into a lake, the ripples will move out in ever-widening circles until the farthest limits are reached. No one can estimate the hidden effect of one such human pebble on the surface of society.

And then the Church, very pointedly *Pope John Paul II: Catechist*, carries a remark of the late Cardinal Danielou that "A solitary Catholic, except by a miracle, will not remain faithful to the Church and to her teaching. It is obvious that he needs the constant support, intellectual and psychological, spiritual and emotional, from his fellow Catholic believers."[8] It is in this environment and only in this environment that a mature Christian can live as fully as possible what he has learned.

How is this environment created? Primarily through an adult community whose members have been instructed through a renewed catechesis geared to their mature Faith. Here the burden rests on those whose responsibility it is to provide such a catechesis. More on that later. However, the supportive effect within a parish family of even a small percentage of well-instructed members is obvious. Good example is catching. To observe the frequent, even daily, devout reception of the sacraments, the intelligent and attentive participation in the liturgy, the warm and sincere expressions of charity in the exercise of the spiritual and corporal works of mercy...all these must have a bolstering effect on those who are striving to make the Gospel a reality in their lives. Such a parish community is blessed indeed.

If the picture drawn of the effects of proper adult catechesis on the family, on society and on the Church or the parish community is to be realized, on whom does the onus rest of making such adult catechesis available? Pope John Paul is most emphatic in his statement of the right of the faithful to receive this instruction and the "duty which the Church has from Christ of providing them with it: this theme, in fact, is the centerpiece of *Catechesi tradendae.*"[9]

Our Holy Father sees the responsibility as being shared by all in the Church beginning with himself as chief pastor, while he enumerates "priests and religious who should find catechesis a preeminent field for their apostolate."[10]

Certainly on a practical level it rests chiefly on the pastor of a parish to make adult catechesis available. No one can know the needs (or no one *should* know the needs) of the adult parishioners better than the one to whom they have been entrusted as a spiritual father. Since Vatican II, every parish has been shaken to its foundations as has been the whole Church. The result has been the loss of numbers of adult parishioners who no longer find in the Church the answers to their questions. Unfortunately, they are seeking answers elsewhere and, perhaps, finding them. In the face of such tragedy can anyone be complacent? Are we satisfied to save the saved? No one doubts the difficulty of the problem; the need exists; the hunger is there. How does one make the hungry soul aware of his hunger? And how does one gently lead the empty seeker to the source where all fullness lies?

First consideration must be given (in an attempt to answer these and like questions) to the intellectual atmosphere in which most of our adults live. With easy access to education in the past thirty years, we have an adult population that expects to be approached on an adult level. Therefore, every consideration must be given to the choice of the catechist, the types of courses, the timing of the courses, the course content, etc., which will appeal to those we are seeking to attract. Only after one has tasted of the spiritual food being distributed is the awareness of his emptiness apparent. Once the appetite has been aroused, there is usually no sating it because the One filling it is infinite.

One may ask, granted the need for adult catechesis, how does one go about making the need a *felt need?* Agreed that a large percentage of adult parishioners suffers from anemic faith, what magic formula can we devise to focus on that weakness and create a desire for a healthy, vigorously-lived faith? "It pays to advertise" is as true in this area as on Madison Avenue. There is nothing more effective in selling a product than a satisfied customer. Therefore, once an attractive adult program has touched the participants and reached deeply into their everyday lives, word will spread and they will return for more, bringing others who have been spurred by their enthusiasm. The "come and see" of Jesus in John 1:39 will echo in every parish where a vibrant, dynamic catechist has begun the renewal called for by Pope John Paul.

In the light of *Catechesi tradendae* let us examine the catechist and the courses mentioned above. Pope John Paul speaks directly of Christ as Teacher, One who taught with authority, the Teacher "Par Excellence." Why? Because it was not only what Christ taught but who Christ was that constituted Him "the Teacher." It was a combination of the doctrine preached and the life lived that made Christ unique. Likewise, the catechist if he or she is to transmit the true message of the Good News must live that Good News in all its ramifications. One cannot give what one does not possess, or as Pope John Paul says: "The person who lives out a catechesis is the best catechist." Only when one has been deeply impregnated by the Gospel message and lives it fully does the sincerity of his teaching touch the deepest core of his listeners. The catechist, then, must not know merely intellectually the doctrines being taught, but must know in the Hebrew sense of knowing, the whole person being caught up into the truth and living by it. As the Holy Father again says:

> The catechetical problem involves more than merely a restoration of "orthodoxy" to catechesis.... It involves, in the profoundest sense, a renewal of the faith of the catechist that will enable him to bear witness through "his life as a whole" to the truths of the Church doctrine which he is enunciating.[11]

The life of the catechist must be a living testament of his dedication to the truths he teaches.

> This is the secret, [he goes on to say] of the relationship of "doctrine and person": the person who believes the doctrine and proves his belief by acting on it in all the acts of his life is the person who will effectively teach the same beliefs and "praxis" to others.[12]

By all means let us have catechists who are trained, who have completed a thorough course in content and method, who have a working knowledge of all the visual aids at hand; but above all and beyond all the mechanics, let us have catechists who are living witnesses of what they teach.

And what should they teach? Here more than elsewhere in his exhortation is the Holy Father most explicit:

> The person who becomes a disciple of Christ has the right to receive the word of faith not in mutilated, falsified, or diminished form but whole and

entire in all its rigor and vigor. Unfaithfulness on some point to the integrity of the message means a dangerous weakening of catechesis.[13]

Therefore, the content of catechesis is not at the whim of the catechist. The Pope declares that no true catechist can pick and choose among the defined dogmas of the Church those he or she prefers to teach.[14] In fact, he presents in one of his most important paragraphs of the document a list of the doctrines that must be included in the authentic teaching of catechesis which the *General Catechetical Directory* likewise enunciates as "the more outstanding elements of the Christian message." Scripture and Tradition head the list as the sources of catechesis.

Fidelity to the teaching authority of the Church, the Magisterium, is the foundation on which the content of catechesis must rest. However, the content must be related to the needs of the recipients. While adhering faithfully to the list of authentic Church teaching, it is imperative that they be applied in all their fullness to the special needs, here and now, of the adults being instructed.

For example: Christology can remain, on an intellectual level, an academic study of the historical Jesus with precise labeling of His miracles, parables, etc. But the authentic Jesus cannot remain in the realm of the abstract, but can and must be presented in the concrete if He is to have any impact on the twentieth century Christian. This magnetic personality must become part of the warp and woof of the fabric of the adult's life as he strives to grow into the fullness of that very Christ. The listener must be led to explore the mind of Christ, His attitudes, His values, His teachings in this effort to make Him visible in the office, the home, the social milieu in which the adult moves. Until all the doctrines and dogmas of the Church become the flesh and blood, the bone and sinew of adult life, they will remain buried in dusty tomes.

Doctrine must be vivified by the life-giving Spirit. The Gospel parable of the seed (the Word of God) dropped on unyielding soil (rock-strewn, hard or thorny) eloquently portrays the fate of catechesis without the work of the Holy Spirit. Pope John Paul was totally aware of the place of the Spirit in all phases of catechetical work:

> Catechesis, which is growth in faith and the maturing of Christian life towards its fullness, is consequently a work of the Holy Spirit, a work that He alone can initiate and sustain in the Church.[15]

Every catechist has the unique privilege of being the mouthpiece of the Spirit, the channel through which the voice of the Spirit vibrates, reaching into the hearts and minds of the hearers. When the catechist is wholly aware of the secondary role he or she plays in relaying the message, an instrument in the hands of the "Master Instructor," of the Spirit who prepares the soil, then and only then will the ground receive the seed yielding a hundredfold. Only the Spirit of Truth can teach all truth. Therefore, if the catechist is to avoid the pitfalls of half truths and outright error so prevalent in our sophisticated age, he or she must be a true disciple of the Spirit, open to His ever-present guidance.

In adult catechesis, more perhaps than in other areas, is the work of the Spirit an absolute. If the mature Christian is to know the mystery of Christ better and better as Pope John Paul teaches, then he must be attuned to the Spirit. His is the work of sanctification, a work culminating in a growth in faith and a maturing in Christ.

Finally, who can measure the sense of fulfillment, the deep satisfaction that is the reward of the catechist engaged in adult catechesis. To witness something of the joy and peace of an adult, once the full meaning of being a Christ-follower dawns on the mature mind, is soul shaking. Once one has experienced confused spiritual lives, crippled by anxiety and fear, developing into confident, loving Christians, one is seized as Paul was "to preach the Gospel in season and out of season." Or as Jeremiah the prophet exclaimed: "There seemed to be a fire burning in my heart, imprisoned in my bones. The effort to restrain it wearied me. I could not bear it."[16]

The need is there, never doubt it. Adult catechesis must reach into every parish to bring the Good News in all its rich fullness to the soul-starved majority. The time is now. The need is urgent. We must heed the call of Pope John Paul:

> All believers have the right to catechesis. All pastors have the duty to provide it.[17]

FOOTNOTES

1. *Catechesi tradendae*, no. 43.
2. National Catechetical Directory, no. 188, p. 113.
3. Gal. 2:20.
4. Phil. 1:21.
5. Jn. 14:6.
6. *Catechesi tradendae*, no. 68.
7. *Apostolicam actuositatem*, no. 6.
8. *Pope John Paul II: Catechist*, no. 24, p. 97.
9. *Ibid.* no. 14, p. 78.
10. *Ibid.* no. 16, p. 80.
11. *Ibid.* no. 5, p. 53.
12. *Ibid.* no. 9, p. 60.
13. *Ibid.* no. 30, p. 118.
14. *Ibid.* no. 30, p. 120.
15. *Catechesi tradendae*, no. 72.
16. Jer. 20:9.
17. *Op. cit.*, no. 64.

CHAPTER FIVE

The Content of Catechesis

Most Rev. Austin B. Vaughan, S.T.D.
Episcopal Vicar
Archdiocese of New York

The topic of this paper is "The Content of Catechesis." It is a topic that touches almost everyone in the Church, in one way or another. It is a matter of concern for a teacher in a parochial school or CCD program who finds herself dealing with textbooks that seem to change every couple of years from what they were before. It is a matter of concern for parents who find themselves puzzled by extensive changes in curriculum, but who usually trust that somebody knows for sure what is happening and where things are going. It is a matter of concern for the children at the age of 13 or 14. What do they need to know now, at that age? What will they need to know 5 years from now? How do we get that across to them effectively? It is a matter of concern to a pastor who finds his efforts to teach his people going in many scattered directions and who is not sure how to pull them together so as to provide guidance for them. It is a matter of concern in a different direction for a theologian who may find his work criticized for having a bad impact on the general public, because critics believe that it confuses people rather than helps them. It is a matter of concern for a bishop who is expected to provide leadership in an age when many things seem to be shifting and many other things are being questioned.

In catechetics, in the last 20 years, we have gone through successive periods of emphasis on salvation history, on relevance, on psychological development in Christian experience, on community action—with strong complaints that each in turn has left doctrinal catechetics impoverished. By hindsight, in each instance it seems that not a great deal has been gained, and a fair number of things of worth that we had seem to have been lost.

I am going to try to approach this topic from the angles of my own experience and competence, which are limited. I am not a catechist as such; I taught 6th grade CCD and I taught religion to Catholic high school girls for the better part of 10 years, but I never considered myself a professional. The nun teaching the 5th grade next door to my 6th grade did a lot better in instructing the children. I have been a theologian for practically all of my adult life—a seminary professor of dogmatic theology. I served on the Board of Ecclesiastical Censors of the Archdiocese of New York for many years; in the 1960's and 1970's, this meant working on catechisms—in fact, in those days, more on catechisms than on anything else, because most of the authors of other Catholic books did not bother to seek an imprimatur, unless in a given instance it would help them commercially. Finally, I have given many talks in parishes in the last 20 years, and I am aware of the reactions of our people in the period of transition after Vatican II; this has been a time of change that has often involved some confusion.

My paper will not be that of a professional catechist, but that of a bishop who is a theologian. I would like to make some remarks on the impact that a number of general theological issues have had on the content of catechesis in our country, and then offer a brief survey of some of the cases where the content of catechesis seems to me to be posing problems in our own country at the present time.

By nature, I am probably problem-orientated. Sometimes when I talk or write, the world may seem to be full of problems. None of the problems that I am going to mention here is insoluble. They are all things that we can do something about. That does not mean that we can expect to have all of the answers completely. But there is nothing here that does not afford us a real possibility for much more clarification than we have now, and for a good deal of movement forward as well.

First, just a little bit of background. In the 1970's, many talks and study-sessions were provided in parishes to update parents on the content and new methods of catechetics. Many of them took place within the context of preparation for their children's first reception of various sacraments, some of them in other areas, such as adult education, or study or discussion groups. At the same time, there were many sessions in seminaries or other locations all over the country to update priests on what had happened in Vatican II and what kind of differences or changes it had produced in the Church. Very often, the impression that was conveyed at that time was that if you knew what the Church or the theologians were trying to do, then your problems and anxieties with regard to the content of catechetics would disappear. Most of the difficulties that some people had with new approaches were attributed to a failure in communication, a lack of understanding on the part of many people as to what was going on. If you knew the background, then the problems would disappear, either because we were simply presenting the old message in a new and more understandable form, or we were searching for a greater and deeper meaning in the same message as before, or we were looking for a way whereby it could have a deeper impact on the lives and the actions of the people who heard it, or—this is a very different direction—we had discovered that some of the things that we had emphasized before were not really as important as we had thought they were. In any case, if you understood what people were trying to do, most of the pieces would fall into place. I do not believe that this was true.

I will come back to this in a moment, but I would like to mention in passing that something very similar happened in areas other than catechetics. In recent years, on several occasions I have heard sisters, giving talks to priests, tell them that many priests did not understand what Vatican II had said and done about religious life; if they had known, they would have had no problems with the changes that had taken place. My problem was that I did know what Vatican II had said and what it intended, and, despite this, I did have problems with a number of the changes, because I do not think they were what Vatican II intended either directly or indirectly. We had something similar happen at times with regard to the liturgy. Many of the liturgical changes brought great benefits to the Church. Not all of them did. And yet often, where they were not a help, the impression was conveyed that, if you understood what they were trying to do, then your problems would disappear. I do not think that this was true.

The area of theology is the one that I was closer to than any of the others. In this area, it seemed to me that an acquaintance with what the theologians were saying, or with what they were trying to do, often—not always— left priests and people more unsettled than when they started. In continuing education courses for priests in the diocese, this was often a problem. They went into the course with the expectation that, at the end of it (often one day a week for two years), they would come out set for the next 20 years, for they would have been updated on what had changed since the time when they left the seminary 20 years before. What happened in many cases was that they had many more problems and questions at the end of the course than they did before they started. I am not saying that this was avoidable, but I am saying that the problem was not just a matter of getting in touch with what was being said in the theological world. It was something more. Sometimes the updating left them more confused than before. And when this happened, some priests would retreat to what they had learned before, feeling a relative degree of safeness and security with that, and confusion when they moved away from it; others began to think that almost everything was questionable, so you were free to go in whatever direction seemed best to you.

What all this means is that there are problems on the level of theology that have a profound effect on the content of catechesis, which have to be faced more effectively than they have been up till now. Let me try to illustrate this by listing five of them, with the understanding that these five do not come close to exhausting the problems in this area. *One* of them: Is revelation truth or is it contact with a person? And, does content really matter? A *second* one: How much pluralism and how much change is possible in the content of catechesis? *Third:* How important is it for the content of catechesis to be relevant? Is this a really significant factor? *Fourth:* What parts of the content of catechesis can you present to Catholics at various ages, or at various cultural levels? And *fifth:* Who should determine the content of catechesis in the post-Vatican II Church? —They may seem rather abstract when they are listed this way, but I do not think that they have been abstract at all, when you measure their concrete impact on our teaching of the Faith on all levels.

The Content of Revealed Truth

On the *first* of them: Is revelation a set of truths, or is it a contact with a Person, with Jesus or with the Holy Spirit? You must have seen that question expressed dozens of times, if not hundreds of times, in the last 15 years. Most of us grew up with the former idea. We described faith as an act of belief, an act of intellectual acceptance of what had been revealed. We accepted the truths that were contained in the Creed. One of the criticisms that was launched against this kind of approach was that it would result in the kind of person who recites the Creed and says that he believes in it, but whose life seems to be completely untouched by it. For him, it is almost like accepting a railroad timetable. He does not deny that what it says is true, but the railroad may be on the other side of the country, and he could not care less. The faith of many people seemed to be akin to this. We recall the old objection that used to be raised about the worth of knowledge of this kind: that a non-Catholic boy or girl could win the religion prize in our schools; what this seemed to prove was that what we were teaching was not particularly significant in terms of commitment or belief.

This criticism went on to say that faith is really an acceptance of Jesus as my Savior, acceptance of a reality that cannot be confined to doctrinal formulas because it reaches out beyond them. A person is much more than a set of propositions; a person touches our whole being and not just the intellect. The commitment that I make to Christ is not just saying "yes" in my mind; instead it means being willing to direct the whole of my life and all of my powers according to what He said. It is true that our previous theology had taught that faith was an act of the intellect *under the command of the will*. But the allegation was made that, practically speaking, not much of anything besides the intellect counted. Hence, the result of the new approach would be to lay new emphasis on the importance of personal contact with Jesus or with the Holy Spirit. I think myself that the criticism of our older approach was valid and justified to a substantial degree. The real contribution that the new approach made was to lay more emphasis on the personal involvement with Jesus on the part of each individual, and on the need for a personal commitment. It brought out the fact that more than our intellect is involved in an act of faith.

So far, so good. The criticism opened up for us the possibility of a deeper understanding of the whole process of faith. But, what created a problem was the failure to integrate this with what was there before. Or, to put it in a different way, how does acceptance of the truths that were revealed by Jesus relate to an acceptance of the person of Jesus or of the Holy Spirit? Both of them are significant. Unfortunately, for some the acceptance of the truths became little more than a symbol of sincerity. What really was important was your own personal relationship to Christ; as for the truths, whatever form they took, they would be one way of approaching Jesus or the Holy Spirit, and if they worked, good for you, and if they did not work, then look for something else. The consequence of this was that many of the truths themselves were not important as long as you maintained a good relationship with Jesus. It was not usually spelled out in precisely those terms but this was the logical row sequence of the approach that was being used.

It is interesting to note that Pope John Paul II, very early in *Catechesi tradendae*, makes it very clear that the object of catechesis, the aim of catechesis, is to know the person of Jesus and to know the teaching of Jesus. You have to have both; the two of them are intermingled and interlocked so that neither one by itself can adequately take care of the other. The reason why it is so important for us to know the message of Jesus is not just out of obedience and it is not out of sympathy with Him and it is not because it adds a nice touch to our devotion to Him. It is because our contact with Jesus Himself, even if it is not wiped out, will at least be blurred and often badly distorted if we do not know the truths that He has revealed. It is easy enough for many people to see Jesus as a kind, self-sacrificing man, and they can gain a good deal from this. But the person who does this is going to miss most of the impact of Jesus if he does not know that He is the Son of God, that He is the Savior of the world, that He is the Messiah promised to the Jews, that He is the one who has redeemed us by the free sacrifice of Himself, who is born of a Virgin, who changed bread and wine into His Body and Blood and rose from the dead and is present upon our altars. The emphasis on contact with Jesus or with the Holy Spirit as a person has led some people to regard truth in statements about Jesus as either unattainable or unimportant, and this ultimately is extremely harmful to our catechesis. It means that we lose the real significance of an intellectual grasp on what He is doing and who He is, and this intellectual grasp is an important part of what makes each one of us a human being.

There are other factors that are involved here. We need a catechesis that is constantly striving for more of the truth and that relates that truth to human living. Let me try to put the same thought in another way. God has not revealed truths to us simply to satisfy our intellectual curiosity. Any approach that lays emphasis on the importance of listing and piling up truths is going to miss what revelation is all about. God has not revealed mysteries just to humble us, just to prove how dumb we are. He does that in passing, if we really need an indication of our limitations. But, He has never revealed a mystery for a purely negative reason. He has revealed truths and revealed mysteries to give us a new vision of human existence.

God became a baby in order to teach us the preciousness of every human being in a way that was deeper and more profound than any simple statement. He did it to bring us into a family relationship with Him, and not just with Himself but with His Mother, which has made our relationship to God and to all other beings more profoundly human and changed it in many respects.

God died on a cross to redeem us, and to instill a great potential for good in all human suffering. There may have been some potential there before, but it was never grasped to any great extent, even among His own people. They felt that suffering was something to be tolerated, to be put up with. Jesus has changed that and transformed it completely. Grasping His revelation is not simply knowing the fact that He died for us on the cross; instead, it is realizing what that death tells us about the potential and the possibilities of all the suffering that takes place in the world, when it is united to Jesus.

God rose from the dead in order to change the whole meaning of death. What He has done is to teach us that physical death is now just a point of transition. For someone who believes in Christ, it no longer has the same kind of horror or the same kind of terrible finality that it had for people through most of the period of the Old Testament.

God was born of a *Virgin* to point up the uniqueness and dignity of women, and to consecrate love by pointing up what is deepest and best in it, in all human loves, including married love. What is deepest and best is a willingness to sacrifice for the sake of someone else. Unity of soul and community of interests are more important than a physical union.

To miss this fuller meaning and implication of the truths that God has given us is to leave revelation unfruitful. If you accept all of the truths that are there, but give no thought to how they apply to our human existence, then your faith will be something that you are holding on to by your finger tips. You will be accepting God's revelation without any realization of why He had bothered to reveal in the first place.

But, on the other hand, to play down or deny the truth that underlies these implications is to destroy their meaning. God *did* become a Man. It is not a beautiful parable. He *did* become a Man in the womb of the Virgin Mary. He *did* die on the cross for us. He *did* rise from the dead.

Now, these examples could go on all day. What I am saying very simply is that the denial or the loss of a part of the truth of revelation results inevitably in a distortion of our picture of God or our picture of man, or of both of them. Part of the reason that some people can dismiss whole areas of revelation and never miss them is that at times we have failed to apply the revealed truths to human existence. This is true for many people with regard to the Blessed Trinity. At least as they perceive it, it would not make a whole lot of difference if they believed that there were five persons in God, or fifteen, instead of three. In point of fact, it would make an enormous difference, because it would be a deviation from a truth that has profoundly transforming effects, if we grasp it not just in terms of there being three Persons in one God, but with a realization of what is implied in that formula: that God is deeply and profoundly Father to us and that this reflects what is at the heart of His being, that Jesus Christ is really and truly God who became Man, that the Holy Spirit that comes to us in the sacraments is God Himself dwelling within us, so that the power of God is present and operative within us. The same thing could be said with regard to the Assumption. Many people have accepted it in almost the same way that they would accept a fact from a railroad timetable on a line they never use: it is true, but it does not seem to make much difference to them. It is very important for us to *apply* the truths of revelation to our lives. But it is also enormously important that what we have to apply be really *truth*, for truth is absolutely necessary to a personal relationship, if it is going to be genuinely human and truly lasting.

Pluralism and Doctrine

Now for a *second* point on the general problem of the content of catechesis—one that affects us in a good number of ways. That content is affected by the question of pluralism of theologies, or, to put it in terms of another aspect of the same thing, by the possibility of development in the doctrine of the Church. This, to me, from a theologian's point of view, still remains the critical theological problem of our time. It has been so for over ten years. I expect that it will be so for another ten, at least. It is not yet adequately solved either in theory or in its implications. What is the problem all about? What is the basis for it, since it crops up everywhere in our catechesis nowadays?

God has given us a *perennial* truth in revelation, something that was true when He revealed it and that will be true if the world goes on for a million years. There is a very real sense in which revelation was given to us completely in the time of the apostles. On the other hand, to be salvific that message has to be incarnated in terms that will relate to people in their historical circumstances. When it was first revealed, it was revealed in a Semitic people in Semitic terms. As the message moved out into the Roman Empire it had to be translated not simply into new words in a different language, but into new concepts and into new categories as well, and that has kept on happening in Church history. It had to be retranslated into Roman terms and then into Gallican terms. Ultimately in our own age, or right after it, it will be retranslated more fully into African or Asian terms. Part of the reason why that can happen is that the reality that is revealed is many-faceted. We never completely and totally exhaust it by any single formulation, so it is and always will be both legitimate and necessary in the Church to seek new formulations.

St. Thomas Aquinas did this in trying to restate the Christian message in terms that would relate to the intellectual currents of his own day. In this sense, there can be development in doctrine. And various ways of expressing the Christian faith can coexist at times. In that sense, we have had various schools of spirituality—(Benedictine, Franciscan, Dominican, etc.), and various schools of theology—(Scotist, Thomist, Suarezian). In the wake of Vatican II, here is where this problem starts for us. Vatican II encouraged us to go back to the beginnings to rediscover values in Scripture or Tradition or even in individual religious communities which may have been set aside over the years, often unwittingly; it also encouraged us to seek new ways to make the message more relevant to our own day. What that led to among theologians was a vast re-examination of doctrine to see how much of what we have is perennial and has to be retained in all times and in all places, and how much may be just one way of expressing the Christian message, a way that might possibly be subject to change. This whole movement has been accentuated especially by questions raised about possible practical changes. We have been living through this for the last fifteen years, and so far there have been no significant changes in the expression of doctrine regarding matters that were taught clearly before, although there are new aspects of doctrine that have been taken up explicitly for the first time.

One example of this kind of re-examination, which attracted great publicity, was the matter of contraception. The critical question that was being asked, from a theological point of view, about birth control, was not "had the Church changed her teaching?" Historical studies made it clear that the Church's teaching was consistent from the first time it came up, at the start of the third century, right down to the time of the death of Pope John XXIII, and there had been no break in the teaching. The question that was raised was: Is it possible that the time has now come for a change on the grounds that the values that were incorporated in that teaching in times past no longer were best presented in terms of that teaching but could be re-presented in a different way? Basically what was being asked was: "Was the Church's prohibition of birth control part of the heart and core of her doctrine or was it just one way of expressing more profound doctrines, a way that was well-suited to ages past but was no longer well-suited to the 20th century?" Pope Paul VI gave the answer to that question and it was the answer that involved an act of discernment using the power that the Holy Spirit had conferred upon him through his office. It said that what was core doctrine or essential was that every act of marital intercourse had to remain open to life and this was not just one way of expressing some deeper truths.

The same kind of questions were raised with regard to the ordination of women: "Is the unbroken tradition of nineteen hundred years the expression of something that God, for profound reasons of His own, wanted to be perennial in the Church, or is it just one way of organizing the Church for a particular age that no longer satisfies the needs of the 20th century?" That question was posed and an answer was given to it in 1977; it was given in a form which seems to me to exclude any real possibility of any change in the future.

The same kind of question has come up in ecumenical discussions in our own day on the possibility of ordination taking place without a bishop, because if the

Church were to allow for this, then the possibility of reunion with a number of churches where there had been no ordinations by bishops would seem to be made simpler, because there would be a much greater possibility of our acknowledging the validity of their ministry. The same question has been raised in some countries in Africa with regard to polygamy. Could the Church accept polygamy because it is part of a given society as a step toward a more complete and total acceptance of the Christian message later on? Those are the kinds of questions that have come up. So far, all of the questions that I have mentioned have been answered in the negative in terms of possibility of change.

The critical problem that is facing all catechetics and all theology is how to be faithful to Christ, and how to be salvific to a new generation and a new world, at one and the same time. How do we reach out with all the powers that God puts into our hands and still make sure that what we are reaching out with is the doctrine of Christ and not a watering down of that doctrine? So far, so good. I think that process is something that we have to live with in terms of incorporating a Christian message in terms that will reach out to a new age, and to new cultures.

But great difficulties have arisen in *two* directions, in the attempt to develop doctrine in a way well-suited to our own times. One of them is a notion of development of doctrine that leaves very little or nothing as permanent except for some vague underlying reality that is expressed by many different formulas in different ages. You adhere to the reality but not to any particular expression of it. On this basis, a number of theologians have advocated and still advocate getting away from the definition of papal infallibility in Vatican I on the grounds that it was fitted to the 19th century political situation but we are not bound to it; or getting away from Chalcedon and its teaching on the Incarnation on the grounds that it is too hemmed-in by a kind of Greek philosophical approach that does not speak to the 20th century; or getting away from Marian doctrines on the Immaculate Conception and the Assumption because they came out of an older cultural setting, the European cultural setting of the 19th century and the early 20th century, that is not binding on other cultures; or getting away from the sexual morality of an earlier age on the grounds that it no longer meets the legitimate aspirations of people in the 20th century. The problem we have here is not a new one. It is a problem that was brought out in Pius XII's Encyclical *Humani generis* in 1950. And the answer that was given then is still an adequate answer. It is the same kind of question that was brought up at the time of the start of the last session of the Second Vatican Council in 1965 when Pope Paul VI put out an Encyclical on the Eucharist called *Mysterium Fidei*. The key point in it is this: We are bound in our belief not just to some vague reality but to what Christ and the Church have said about it. We are bound to truths, to propositions, to statements that have incorporated or represented that reality as far as they were able to do so at that time. What that means is that it is always possible for the Church to add to defined doctrinal statements, but she cannot discard any of their positive contents. Now that sentence seems simple, but I believe it is not accepted by a good number of theologians in our day. And it makes a critical difference, because it really pins down the extent to which we really are committed to the definitions that have come from the past. I think this is the Church's own understanding of the axiom that what has once been defined always remains defined. Revealed truth is never exhausted, so there is always the possibility, at least in some cases, of saying more about the same thing. But the something more can never contradict what was positively said before. I think that this point is critical to our theology and our catechetics.

The second difficulty that has come up in this area is a notion of pluralism that allows for contradictory positions in our theology or catechetics. Sometimes, this is cloaked over by vagueness, but it is accepted on a fairly wide basis. It is often suggested as a solution to our ecumenical problems. The way to reunite is to take some of the doctrines that are more peripheral and put them on a shelf. We will continue to believe them. The other people who unite with us will not believe them even though they are defined. They are not that important. That kind of position was already condemned in the 1973 Declaration of the Congregation for the Doctrine of the Faith entitled: *Mysterium Ecclesiae,* but it still persists as a real proposal. It is often proposed as the solution to the problem of dissent from the official teaching by Catholic theologians: instead of being monolithic, we have to be pluralistic and allow for a number of different positions. It is often proposed more popularly in the form of a saying: "We don't have all the answers like we used to think we did." Or "it is more important for us to search than to find." Now a constant search for a greater grasp on the reality of the universe is good, if what that means is that we never believe that we have got it all, and so, there is always something more to look for.

An openness to whatever is real is good. But, the implication of accepting the coexistence of contradictory positions is to say that either nobody knows the truth in this instance or that the truth does not make any difference. The idea of a search for truth is fine, but the remark that was made half a century ago by Gilbert Chesterton still applies. He said that the purpose of an open mind in some ways is very much like that of an open mouth: it is to close it again on something solid. It is important for us to pursue truth and we do it with an awareness that we never arrive at it completely. Even our common sense tells us that. Anyone with any sense or brains knows that he does not know it all. But if he thinks he can know nothing for sure, maybe it would be better for him to give up the effort. You just cannot live or operate or even breathe for any length of time if you are really proceeding on that basis.

The question of what pluralism is legitimate, and what pluralism undermines the effective teaching of the Christian message is a vital one for the Church both in theology and catechetics. I think that is obvious. But despite the fact that it is obvious, you constantly will find people speaking of the desirability of pluralism and going right past this concomitant question which is all important. Unless this question is faced squarely and surely on the level of theology it will be impossible to provide a solid and secure catechetics. That does not mean that catechetics will have to have all the answers, but it will have to have enough of them to make it worth pursuing and paying attention to. We are affected by this now in our own country. Some areas, it seems to me, are virtually ignored in catechetics. The obvious one is sexual morality because of the impact of dissent. This does not mean that our catechisms are going to print things that are directly or admittedly contrary to the teaching of the Church. There would be no imprimatur on them if they did, in most cases. What it means—and I think this is well-intentioned but it can be just as harmful, even though it is well-intentioned—is this: because of the notion of pluralism and because of the fact that there is dissent, there is very little desire or enthusiasm to emphasize points that seem to be disputed by theologians, and hence to be unsure. This has had a lot of impact, and I will come back to it later.

Relevance and Catechesis

A *third* kind of general question: the content of catechesis has been affected by emphasis on the *relevance* of doctrine. Now once again, this comes from a good and legitimate desire to make revelation generally salvific (to reach people). Pope John Paul II, in a talk in Ireland, touched on the method of catechizing and evangelizing and said that bringing the faith to a new generation is like discovering a new continent. You have to look for new approaches that will make it real and that will get through to them. The risk involved is that seemingly relevant items may be taken up with almost no background or rooting in the Faith being provided. That happened in our catechesis in the 60's when it moved into an emphasis on relevance: a lot of discussion on sex, a lot of discussion of social action, a lot of discussion of whatever teenagers wanted to discuss, but without its being tied in very clearly with any kind of concept of the whole Christian message. Ultimately you wind up going nowhere.

A greater risk even than that is that much of Christian doctrine will be ignored because its relevance is not obvious. We are down to the question of whether all of the doctrine that counts even at a given moment is just the doctrine that is "relevant." John Paul II, in *Catechesi tradendae*, is very strong on the necessity of presenting the whole of our doctrine. Integrity in doctrine. You do not leave any parts of it out completely. And there is a reason for that, or a couple of reasons. One of them is that many things are relevant without our realizing it, because our teaching is organic. One part ties in with another and affects it very, very profoundly. I think religious discovered this in the 60's and 70's in the case of many of the questions that were raised about the significance of the meaning of poverty and chastity and obedience. A lot of things were put aside or dropped entirely because no one succeeded in showing how they were relevant now. Sometimes we discover that things (or, for that matter, people) were relevant, only after they are gone.

There is a famous true story from our own day of Thor Heyerdahl, the man who built the raft "Kon-Tiki" to cross the Pacific. You may recall that after he had shown that he could get across the Pacific on a raft to show how populations might have moved, he decided to see if he could get across the Atlantic from Africa on a papyrus boat, to try to prove that the Egyptians might have done it long ago. So he made a papyrus boat. And he made it just to the image of papyrus boat pictures portrayed in the pyramids. And in the course of building it—he admitted this later—they found an extra rope on the back of the boat. They could not see any purpose for it at all and they figured that it was an extra decoration and they did not want anything extra, so they left that rope off. They took off from West Africa, got out about 25 miles and discovered why that rope had been in the picture. If you have a paper or papyrus boat, it gets water-logged in the back and it is going to get pulled down unless there is something holding it up. They sank 50 miles off the coast of Africa. He went back and built another boat and this time he put in a rope. The only reason for mentioning this is that it is worth keeping in mind that there are many things in our lives that have relevance, especially things that have been there for a long time, maybe for a generation or two before us, whose relevance we have forgotten or never knew. Another example: I know good, well-intentioned people who, when *Humanae vitae* came out, opposed it on the grounds that they thought that birth control was perfectly acceptable for married couples in some instances, even though they did not favor any other kind of changes in our sexual morality—just that one. They refused to see that if you admitted the principle that a person could, for a good reason, decide to use marital intercourse apart from any connection with the origin of human life, then people could come up with other good reasons to use it apart from marriage completely. The same people who, in 1968, said they would never go a step farther than that, by 1976 were accepting, on a selective basis, homosexuality, premarital intercourse and adultery in some instances where it seemed to benefit the parties. Ultimately, the implications of something that seemed to have very limited relevance went far beyond it.

There is another thing that is involved here: because relevance is something that can shift with times and places, something that seems to be important in 1981 may look different in 1990. To offer an example of that from my own experience: back in 1954, I gave a talk at Columbia University on the Church's teaching with regard to our Lady, to an audience which was made up to a great extent of students from Union Theological Seminary. It was right after the time, in a different ecumenical climate, when the Presbyterian General Synod had attacked our Mariology as a distortion of the Christian message and as putting Mary in place of the Holy Spirit. I tried to explain our Mariological doctrine, and the audience raised no great objection to most of the teaching except for the definition of the dogma of the Assumption in 1950. They could not understand why it had taken place because it seemed to be divisive. If the Pope really cared about Protestants, why did he not leave this matter, which had no significance, off to the side. I could not point out to them any immediate relevance in 1954. The Holy Father had said he had done it for the greater glory of the Trinity and to pay honor to our Lady, but you could not turn that into something that simply had to be done at that time. I could not describe the relevance of the doctrine in any urgent terms. Now, twenty years later, I have no difficulty in doing so. We have moved into a period in which many people have serious doubts about the existence of the future life for anyone besides Christ, and where they have extremely distorted ideas of the resurrection of the body. I think that particular doctrine was defined, in God's intentions, at that particular period precisely to be in place for the period that came after. The other thing that that doctrine did was to indicate very clearly that the basis for our acceptance of doctrine was and would continue to be not merely scripture taken by itself on the basis of a literal exegesis, but the Church's own understanding of the full Christian message as it developed in the course of time. With that background we could develop ecumenical relationships with other churches, without being in danger of falling into a "scripture alone" kind of approach. Now that is just an example. The search for relevance is good but it has to be worked into a complete presentation of revelation.

The Question of Psychological Development

A *fourth* kind of general problem, and I think many of you are better acquainted with this matter than I am: the content of catechesis has been affected by stress on the psychological development of youngsters; this is an area in which I do not feel any competence, but where I do feel some of the pains created by this approach. Back as far as ten years ago, Brother Gabriel Moran disappointed many of the people in the field of catechesis who had put their trust in him when he finally reached a position where he said that no kind of abstract concept should be presented to any youngsters before the ages of 14 or 15. They could not handle it. The result was that the teaching of dogma in our ordinary sense should be forgotten about and put aside. What that has meant in catechisms is that a doctrine like original sin should not be taught or presented in the early grades, on the grounds that this is a kind of concept that these youngsters cannot cope with. In practice, it has been one of the main reasons for putting off First Confession until 11 or 12, on the grounds that, before that, youngsters are not able to grasp the idea of sin in a meaningful way, and so we are giving them a wrong or a false orientation by introducing it earlier. More recently, emphasis on the process of values clarification instead of imposing of values on others has been based on a particular theory of psychological development.

The area where this concerned me most often in the past was as a censor of catechisms. It is something that was a real headache. I can and I could tell if a statement of doctrine were true, false, or ambiguous. What I could not judge, with my limited competence, was the correctness of someone who would come along and say that this should be omitted for psychological or pedagogical reasons: the child is too young to handle that. I am not an expert on the mental abilities of small children. And I suspect I was in the same boat with practically anybody else who was censoring catechisms at that time. We often passed things that did not specifically mention certain doctrines, and we would often get violent reactions from parents, among others, who would say: "How can you allow this kind of thing to go on?"

We still need clear, pastoral judgments on what can and should be taught, that involve the insights of parents, teachers, psychologists, theologians, as well as our own recent pastoral experience and the pastoral experience of the Church in centuries gone by. The ultimate decisions have to be made by the Bishops and the Pope. But this is not an area where they start out with an acquired knowledge of their own or with a defined dogma. Our confusion over the age for First Confession was partly due to the fact that we did not, at an earlier stage, address more directly the question of what psychological conclusions or theories are compatible with the Faith and the practice of the Church and which are not. Because the psychological development of children does have impact on the content of catechesis, it is too important to be left to psychologists alone. In a sense, this is obvious, because it affects all of us. I do not feel personally competent in this area. But it is one that we have to deal with more directly than we had to in the past.

Catechetics and Hierarchy

Finally, the last general problem: the content of catechesis has been affected by disputes over who determines what is the content of catechetics and how—and over what this says about what should be said and taught right now. The official Church is not confused on this, but what she has taught in this regard is not universally and maybe not even generally accepted by those who do most of the writing. In the recent past, what should be taught was decided by the official teachers of the Church, the Pope and Bishops in their pronouncements.

That was supported inevitably by a consensus of theologians who worked in agreement with the Pope and Bishops in expressing doctrines. Some things were taught that everybody agreed upon, and the things where there were legitimate disputes were set aside in other works. It seems to me that the catechisms of that time were conservative in the things they presented. They were slow to move in new directions until the new positions were firmly established.

Now, a number of factors have affected this in our own day. Many older doctrinal positions are questioned by theologians. We no longer have a doctrinal consensus. Even on the most fundamental doctrines, if you want to find somebody to disagree, you can do so. I had a discussion with one of the more prominent theologians in our country within the past two weeks in which he said that in a particular writing he had expressed clearly a consensus position on virginal conception. I said "it seems to me that you haven't accepted the physical reality of the virginal conception." He said that was true. He accepts virginal conception but he accepts it as a symbol for the Incarnation or for the holiness of Mary. Well, maybe that is acceptance, but it is not acceptance of the way that the doctrine has been universally accepted in the past, nor is it an acceptance that I could go along with as adequate. There are a number of factors that have contributed to this. I mentioned the doctrinal positions questioned by theologians.

A second factor is that more emphasis has been laid on the practical aspects of studying doctrine, translating it into action and having an impact on peoples' lives. This has been going on for about 10 to 15 years, depending on the theologian involved. The result of it is that theologians are not content to keep new positions to themselves until they are carefully tested. That is where we would have been 20 years ago, but that is not where we are at now. The testing, if there is to be any testing, goes on in the public forum rather than the private. The development of communications media has made new theories readily available to the public. It is not an accident that they get to that area. Now, that has resulted in a claim for two magisteriums at least in practice, and sometimes in theory as well. On the one hand, we have officially proposed teaching and, on the other hand, we have positions of theologians that sometimes go well beyond official teaching and sometimes contradict it. Which should serve as the source for the content of catechesis? I do not think that there is any question at all that, by right, the answer should be the teaching of the Pope and the Bishops. That teaching should be kept current with regard to significant questions so that it is responding to the difficulties that are raised. But, in practice, what we very often wind up with as the content of catechesis are only those matters where Bishops and theologians agree; the rest of the matters are either glossed over, or else the notion of pluralism and the acceptability of completely opposed and divergent views is presented. What that does is to weaken our catechesis, to minimalize it. It is reduced only to the things where there is universal agreement, and that is not a whole lot in our own day, and it cuts down on what is genuinely thought of as important.

In this area we need more involvement on the part of the hierarchy in what is being taught on the level of catechesis and in the ideas that are being propounded through the media. And we need a clear assertion that the ultimate act of discernment on what is to be taught, in Jesus' intentions, lies with the Pope and the Bishops. We have to face the fact that our catechesis, on some levels at least, has to be more responsive to the questions that are being raised about the Catholic Faith. What that means is we need a new and updated apologetics in the broad sense of the term, a response to the kind of objections that are being raised today. We also have to achieve a greater unity in this catechesis. There are many areas where there are significant differences of a contradictory nature in what is being taught right now or where certain teachings are significantly omitted.

I intended to go on from here to list some areas where the content of our catechesis is currently a matter of concern—where the problems I mentioned earlier have had an impact on what is taught or not taught—and on how this teaching affects religious practice and moral life. I have 35 topics listed in 4 categories, but this list is not a complete one; you can expand upon it yourselves. Because I have already spoken a long time, I won't go through them now—but some of them would be obvious: —original sin, the necessity of baptism, the humanity of Jesus, and the extent of His human knowledge, the existence of hell and purgatory, the reality of mortal sin, contraception, divorce and remarriage, the inspiration of Scripture and its historicity and its inerrancy (which, after reformulation of doctrine, is, I think, the most critical doctrinal question at the present time). We could go on all day with these, but there is no time to do it now.

Just to conclude: What is it that the Church needs in the area of content in catechesis in our day? Just to start, the biggest problem in catechetics in the United States, it seems to me, is not directly one of content. It is the people we are missing. The people we never get to at all in catechesis. The numbers somebody wrote about a few years back, about the lost 6 million children who disappeared from any of the lists of CCD and from any kind of religious education program of Catholic schools. Move it up to the secondary level and the numbers increase and the proportion missing is much bigger than in grade school. That is not directly a question of content, but indirectly I believe that it is. The lack of the sense of urgency to communicate what we have is due, I think, to what happened to the content of our catechesis. It is an interesting kind of parallel, for me: in the county I am in now, there is a big drive on the part of a number of people to upgrade and improve our marriage preparation. The reason for that is that they are horrified at the increase in the number of broken marriages and divorces especially among those who marry very young. And the reaction is: "We have got to do something about it. We cannot let this go on." So, there is a great deal of ferment on improving the programs. There is not that kind of ferment about the importance of reaching those we are not reaching now with catechetical programs and I think there is a doctrinal basis for it. There is not the same sense that souls will be lost if they are not catechized and if the truth does not reach them. God will take care of them anyway and the truth does not really make that much of a difference at all.

The second biggest problem I think we have in catechetics is confusion over what is Catholic teaching on many points in the light of new challenges, with a consequent feeling that belief is not very important because truth is either unattainable or not significant.

The third is one that I mentioned before: there is a need for apologetics on a popular level. We have to get intelligent people operating and producing responses to the questions and challenges that are already here and still coming. Part of the fault here is the failure of many of us in the last decade to respond concretely to challenges that can be answered, to arguments that can be demolished in some instances, but where not much has been done.

And finally there is a need for more application of our truths to life-situations. There are many doctrines which, due to our fault, are believed but become relatively insignificant, not because God made them insignificant or because they do not count, but because we have not given serious attention to how they apply to us. This symposium is a good sign of concern for the full reality of what God has revealed, and offers great possibilities for the years ahead to go more deeply into that.

CHAPTER SIX

Who Is Going To See to It That Young Catholics Are Taught What It Means To Be a Good Catholic?

Rev. Msgr. George A. Kelly
Director
Institute for Advanced Studies in Catholic Doctrine
St. John's University, New York

No matter how you ask this question, a correct answer has to be a matter of major importance to anyone who believes in the Catholic Faith and the Catholic Church.

Let me put the question in other ways. Are young Catholics being taught to say "Credo" to the Faith to which they were committed at baptism by parents and godparents? Are they growing in faith with each year's association with the Church's commissioned teachers? Are they learning—even if not always practicing—what it means to be a good Catholic? Do they believe what the Church teaches? Do they live by that teaching?

The answer to all these questions ought to be yes, even though it does not always work out that way. How else can we explain the half-educated Catholics and religious illiterates who have been and still are commonplace in the Church? Of one thing, however, we can be certain: the Church has always wished the answer to all those questions to be yes. From the Apostles' Creed through the *Didache* to Augustine's *De Catechizandis Rudibus* to the *Catechism of the Council of Trent* until the *Baltimore Catechism* and Cardinal Gibbon's *Faith of*

Our Fathers were no longer adequate, the presumption of catechesis has been that a Catholic's initial act of faith will be deepened in a learning process *(fides quarens intellectum)*, that catechumens and catechezands will as a result of training come to know what their Faith means and what it demands of them. In the American context, for example, Catholic high school graduates were expected to know the essentials of the Catholic creed and how they personally measured up to its standards. If the catechesis was really effective they also were to care about their failures and shortcomings—both in faith and/or morals.

Up until 1962 the Church in the United States received high marks not only for its successful catechesis of immigrants, but for the high quality of its Catholic life, including that of its youth. Pius XII and John XXIII, especially, were admirers of the faith and religious practice of the American Catholic community.

The Contemporary Catholic Problem

Twenty years after the opening of the Council that was to turn out even better Catholics, the Church's youth no longer practice the Faith like their parents did when they were young. And they do not seem to know the specifics of what their supposed faith demands of them or why. Nor do they believe in the Catholic Church as strongly as earlier generations of American youth did. Opinion polls (reported at a national meeting of Catholic educators) even indicate that Catholic schools today have little or no effect on what students think about sex, marriage or prayer.

We are not talking here of a generation gap. Nor of a passing maladjustment to post-Vatican II changes in Church policies. If this were the case, the slippage could be viewed as a temporary statistical downturn in an otherwise normal upward curve line.

The present situation, however, seems different, and by all accounts (extending over fifteen years) it begins to look serious. Increasingly, pastors speak of eighteen-year-olds who graduate from Catholic high schools not knowing the content and meaning of standard Catholic terms. Incoming Catholic college students have very unclear ideas about eternal life, grace, and the sacraments—in spite of twelve years of Church schooling. Many of them cannot distinguish between the Old and New Testament, and a large number have no appreciation of miracles, what the resurrection of the dead means, or even the purposes of marriage. A campus minister at the Harvard-Radcliffe Catholic complex recently spoke of the "intense hunger" today's incoming students have for "an informed faith." She saw the work ahead of her as exciting. ("There is no end to what needs to be done.") Why is her work exciting? Because students "come with faith but it's an uninformed faith"—the result of a diffused and inadequate content in their earlier religious education programs. She does not address the larger problem, of course, viz., that, while she is dealing with scores of Catholic freshmen and women, the Catholic graduates of high schools can be measured in the thousands.

At lower levels parents watch their fourteen-year-old sons and daughters finish eight years of Catholic elementary school without having gone to confession more than a few times since their First Communion. These teenagers move on to high school often without a sense of need for penance and without knowing how to conduct themselves during confession. This should not be surprising when we find that primary grade youngsters are now conditioned, even by comic strips published by a N.Y. missionary society, to learn early that being sorry for sin is important, not confession. In the comic strip, for example, the children are told that the priest's blessing at the beginning of Mass was the way sins were forgiven in the first 700 years of the Church, as if that reading of history was correct or a controlling matter for present-day Catholics.

Response of Religious Educators

There is no universal response, of course, but many religious educators are defensive about the reported shortcomings of the products of modern catechetics. They express their feelings in a variety of ways. Those who have given up believing that there is anything especially divine about Catholic Christianity look upon the statistical shifts as a long-overdue accommodation to the secular reinterpretation of Christianity. Ecumenicists think the Church's stress on "orthodox" belief is too narrow a focus in an era dedicated to bridging religious differences. Devotees of pluralistic Catholicism think that the present tendency to de-emphasize unity in worship, ministry, or theological formulations represents a return to an early form of Christianity, even if it is less tidy a one than the Catholicism to which they became accustomed after Trent.

A response popular with educators who wish to stand above the present theological controversies is that, since the Church is in the process of redefining what it means to be a good Catholic, old standards of judgment about this are no longer valid. Following a national convention of Catholic educators a leading spokesman for the group indicated that the shift from stress on external manifestations of other-world values (Sunday Mass, no divorce, etc.) to new post-Vatican II concerns for the development of "just, peace-loving, social-minded, chaste Catholics" is already in process. The difficulty, as he saw it, is that we cannot be sure how the new emphasis will work out in practice. Hence the best that educators can do for the moment is to help students cope with change and "to teach the students their personal responsibility to seek the truth and to act in accord with it."

That this approach is widely accepted among Catholic educators (and has its effect on their thinking) is reflected in a recent report published by one large diocesan newspaper of a high school study conducted by the local school office. When the students were asked to arrange four topics in order of importance to their own religious needs, freshman girls rated basic religious teachings first, while the juniors and seniors placed the basic teachings last. All the boys from first to fourth year listed issues of justice and peace as their first religious priority with basic teachings coming in last. The report suggested that "religion classes once criticized for being a series of canned questions and memorized answers are taking the fundamental teachings of the Church and applying them directly to the situations students meet in their daily lives." Asked to offer suggestions for the future, some of the boys were reported as saying:

> Know and experience Jesus now. (Don't go back to what he used to be like.)

It is at this precise point that other questions arise. Can young Catholics find truth if they are not taught truth? Are newly-trained Catholics really applying Catholic principles to their lives?

The Rise of "Experiential" Catechesis

Almost by the opening of the Second Vatican Council religious educators were setting in place throughout the Catholic system a more dynamic way of presenting Christianity. The proposed new emphasis turned away from questions and answers about doctrine and law, away from abstract presentations about the Church's ancient problems, toward proclaiming Christ and His Gospel in personal terms which made sense to modern men and women. The name that was given to this approach was "experiential catechesis." A recent pastoral letter of an American Archbishop explains what it means:

> Experiential catechesis is teaching in dialogue with life. This kind of teaching not only examines life experiences; it also gives meaning to human situations and sheds light on them. Experiential catechesis does this by reflecting on human experience in the

light of the gospel teachings, Catholic doctrine, Christian witness, liturgical celebrations, the history of salvation and of Church tradition. Catechetical fidelity demands constant interplay between these teachings and our experiences of life.

Formal instruction is expected to occur but the Archbishop's pastoral reasserts more than once that catechesis is more than passing on information and abstract truth, more than an exercise in modifying human behavior. The purpose of catechesis, it says, is to get people to know God, not simply to know about God.

In many ways experiential catechesis is radically different from the catechesis traditional in the Church from time immemorial. The new catechists do not suggest that earlier religionists failed to know God. They simply assert that they encourage young Catholics (and others) to know their Faith (i.e., God) by "personal experience" freely sought and freely felt, as distinguished from earlier methods which used techniques of "Church indoctrination"—routine, memorization, discipline. Earlier methods did achieve certain measurable effects (e.g., high rates of Mass attendance) but in too many instances "the religion" was external and socially induced, lacking the personal encounter with God which is the very substance of the Beatific Vision itself.

The Archbishop's pastoral does not go into the subject in great depth but—beyond the encounter element which is important to the faith experience—there are certain underlying concepts to this approach which must be understood if the method itself is to be evaluated properly. Experiential catechesis is based on the conviction that revelation is an ongoing reality which happens whenever people are attentive to God's word. Religious things are not those which happened a long time ago, but are present-day encounters with God. People's own experience—including that of children—is the important locus of religious reflection. Two basic intellectual concepts underpin this approach to catechesis: doctrinal abstractions, especially if taught to children, are not helpful in the modern world for personal religious experience; it is sounder psychologically to lead people to God from what they know naturally (induction) than having them try to apply official declarations or traditional formulas of the Church to their unique life situation (deduction). These presumptions, it is said, flow directly out of the modern findings of religious psychology and sociology.

There is also an important theological (or faith) dimension to experiential catechesis. Again, an unproved principle justifies the methodology: Revelation no longer is seen simply as God's communication with man, nor as ending with Christ and the last Apostle. (Some would see God's ongoing revelation as discoverable [evolving] in other traditions beside the Judaeo-Christian.) The Bible is to be viewed as an account of the felt religious experience of the Jewish people, of how through the ages they developed their particular relationship with God. These sacred books contain a time-conditioned story of a religious people working out their human problems at particular stages of ancient history. It is also the story of God working out His Providence through those struggles and in collaboration with the people themselves. Contemporary Christians must recognize that even today mankind's ongoing relationship with God is dynamic not static, that God is working out His plans today as He did many times before, even as man himself is continuing to evolve toward new stages of development. Consequently, the Bible (and Church tradition) are better seen, not as blueprints for modern man, but as guidelines which still need individual application. Previous answers by religious authorities to old problems are to be respected but they are also to be examined critically, much the way modern biblical scholars study the Bible or modern theologians analyze Church documents—for the lessons they convey. But those lessons are not absolutely controlling because human experience never stands still. There are no final answers to human problems, not even religious answers, because the problems are never the same.

Unquestionably, the experiential approach to Catholic catechesis is modern and, one might add, very American. It has dominated public education for the better part of this century. Because it involves students and "their" contribution to the learning process, it has the ring of democracy. It also fits comfortably into a culture which accentuates the individual, self-fulfillment, and personal decision-making. Avoiding the appearance of seeming to impose, the methodology entices a learner to reach his own answers and those which satisfy him. Hopefully with direction they will be right answers, too. Experiential techniques applied to catechetics have led to interesting, attractive and professionally written textbooks. Visual aids and workshop formats have proved to be better received than tedious lectures. In addition, the search for meaningful religious learning has resulted in lively liturgical celebrations, family participation in parish sacramental programs, renewed interest in adult catechesis, and involvement of the "people of God" in what for too long was looked upon as an exclusive priestly or religious enterprise. One veteran of the catechetical circuit recently wrote that today's young are better educated religiously than their parents!

Only a man from Mars could be blind to the gains made in religious educational techniques, especially from the useful humanistic/ecumenical components to a catechesis which hitherto was completely other-world oriented—at least at the lower levels of Catholic education. Doctrinal purists tend to down-play these gains, even though there is basis in Vatican II for all of them.

However, the doctrinal purists are not without valid points of their own; ignorance of concepts, data, and norms is not acceptable in other forms of study or behavior; rationalizations for illiteracy do not justify it; improved methodology must improve knowledge or behavior if its value is to remain unquestioned. Furthermore, teaching/learning is more than a psychological performance; it is a social process. It involves social structure, beginning with the family. The original *tabula rasa* is filled up with impressions—early. Repetition, once venerated as the mother of learning, is still an important element in reinforcement of learning habits necessary for living in society. Even judgments about success or failure in teaching or learning are made by society. "Personal experience" can be satisfying but also deviant; and if religious, it need not be Christian. It is not Christian if it is unrelated to what Christ and the Church teaches. Finally, new code words like *human enrichment, pastoral concern, freedom of conscience,* which are psychological values, must fit into the socialization process called evangelization and reconciliation. They are helpful if they actually convert catechumens or reconcile sinners to Catholicism. If they serve to diminish the necessity and meaning of faith as defined by the Catholic Church, then these code words become tools to tear down, rather than build up, the Church which by faith is Christ's living body.

Another Look at the Catholic Creeds

These concerns explain why a new look is being given to what is commonly called "doctrinal catechetics," that method almost consistently used to train converts from the beginning of the Church. As late as 1979 in *Catechesi tradendae* John Paul II said it is quite useless to abandon the "serious and orderly study of the message of Christ in the name of a method concentrating on life experience" (no. 22). He made this statement out of the Church's conviction that Christ's truth cannot be discovered by private experience, even though at some point the Christian message must be integrated with people's lives. Vatican II called priests "instructors in the Faith" *(On Priests,* no. 6). The *General Catechetical Directory* calls for the development of faith "through the light of instruction" (II, 17), and John Paul II reminds us that the Catholic Creeds, including Paul VI's *Credo of the People of God,* "bring together the essential elements of the Catholic Faith, especially those that presented greater difficulty or risked being ignored" (CT, no. 28).

The doctrinal method of catechetics, even though looked upon as antiquarian, intermingled with unnecessary pieties and doomed to failure in a here-and-now secular world, is based on its own fundamental assumption: viz., that there is a message of salvation to be conveyed as true to those who believe in Christ. As Christ sent Apostles to guarantee His message for the first generation of Christian converts, so the Church through Pope and Bishops—the chief catechists—must also insist on teaching the content of an objective, once and for all revelation given to men by God through Jesus Christ. Individual believers surely respond to that message in a personal way and there is no reason for the catechesis to be dull or the learning of its meaning tiresome. But content to that message there must be. Even secular pedagogues realize now, as universally they once did, that something must be given before something can be gotten. The shortcomings in secular education based on experimental programming are only too evident not to demand a more integrated methodology for handing on the Catholic Faith.

Increasingly, Bishops themselves are coming to see that some balance must be restored to the catechetical process—that learning, indoctrining, formation of character, routine, ritual, and Catholic discipline are necessary. The Bishops are in search of a new deal in catechetics because the experiential methodology intended to produce a more rounded Catholic has weakened the ties of many Catholics to their baptismal faith instead. The Church's hierarchy has been confessing a need for return to some basics. How does one explain otherwise the succession of official documents? First came the *General Catechetical Directory* from Rome (1971), followed shortly by the American Bishops' *Basic Teachings* (1973), and then by consultations over several years which led to the *National Catechetical Directory* (1977). Paul VI, acknowledging the world-wide dimensions of the problem, insisted that catechetics be made the exclusive theme of the 1977 Synod of Bishops. This Synod prepared the way for John Paul II's Apostolic Exhortation *Catechesi Tradendae* (October 16, 1979) which sought to solidify once and for all the Christian Faith and life of those who are catechized by the Church (CT, no. 4).

One would think, after all these official statements, that the Church's catechetical practices and views would have proceeded to go where hierarchy wished them to go. Yet, ten years after the *First International Catechetical Congress* (September 25, 1971), Catholicism is still no closer to a satisfactory post-Vatican II catechesis, certainly not in the West. Indeed, things are getting worse. If Catholics forty years of age and over were withdrawn from Sunday Mass statistics, our Churches might be judged to be relatively empty of the products of experiential catechesis. Even the views of aging Catholics on right and wrong, and on articles of Faith (resulting in part from what they hear from their children, in part from what they see in their parishes or read in the Catholic press), are not so clearly Catholic as they once were. Nor are the confessional lines any longer than in times past.

Now, two years after *Catechesi tradendae* was issued, the Prefect of the Congregation of the Clergy in charge of the Church's world-wide catechetical effort spoke of "the dramatic falling off" in religious observance and of the rise of "sins against humanity." In explaining the origin of these problems, Silvio Cardinal Oddi cited "present day catechetical excesses" and attacks on "the very fundamentals of our Faith" from within the Church itself. He recalls John Paul II entreating Rome's parish priest missionaries "to begin all over again from the very beginning of the faith." Why should we begin all over as if we were engaged in a new enterprise? Because, said the Pope, "the *majority* of Christians today *(his emphasis)* feel bewildered, confused, perplexed and even misled by widely disseminated ideas that contradict revealed truth."

These are serious charges by the no. 1 and no. 2 catechists of the Church. They represent unusual candor about the failure of hierarchy ("the priest is the central figure in the catechetical apostolate"—Cardinal Oddi) to teach the Faith effectively.

In his New York appearance in the spring of 1981, Cardinal Oddi made two references to *Catechesi tradendae* which have a bearing on our contemporary problem. One was to the teaching of the Church "that the fullness of the revealed truths and of the means of salvation instituted by Christ is found in the Catholic Church" (no. 32). The second reference was to his identification of catechesis with God's revelation "transmitted by the universal magisterium of the Church in its solemn or ordinary form" (no. 52). The first point deals with the centrality of the institutional Church itself to salvation, the second with the substance of God's Word in the Church's catechesis.

Acceptance of these two claims of and by the Church are essential to any authentic transmission of the Catholic Faith. The kerygma of Christ comes to citizens of the twentieth century world only through the living Church they see and hear. Only through the voices of ministers commissioned as successors of the Apostles do they hear the authentic word of Christ. The first Apostles, it must be remembered, were commissioned by Christ, who was also sent, so He said: "I came, not of my own accord, but he sent me" (Jn. 8:42). Again: "As the Father has sent me, even so I send you" (Jn. 20:21). (The fourth evangelist speaks of Jesus having been sent by the Father forty-two times.) The only guarantee, therefore, that the faithful have about Christ's words is the authority of those who were sent by Christ. If these ministers fail to deliver the message, then the message will *never* be delivered in its full or proper form. No amount of personal study will give them the sureness of faith, no delving through library shelves, no deep meditative process will ever validate Christ or His message—if they do not believe or come to believe that the living voice of Christ is the Church and that its voice is true.

Growing Disbelief in the Church

Disbelief in the Christ of history begins today as it always did with disbelief in the Living Christ which is the Church. Christ Himself warned about this—against false teachers, how they would prove to be obstacles to the faith of His little ones, and about the lawlessness they would engender (Mt. 7 and 18). Yet little is being done to resist or counteract the denigration of the Church in our time not only as the *embodiment* of Christ but as the *voice* of Christ.

The reasons why contemporary catechesis is and has been failing can be summarized under two headings.

1. *Priests and religious educators are denigrating the Catholic Church as the Body of Christ.*

2. *Priests and religious educators are casting doubts on Revelation, the Church's origins and the authenticity of Catholic teachings.*

1. Attacks on the Institutional Church

The word *attack* is not too strong a word to describe what has gone on since the opening of Vatican II. The Council was convoked to re-form the structures of Catholicism (laws, priorities, hierarchies, orders, customs, etc.) in order that the Body of Christ become a more appealing Minister in our time to His Word and His Grace. In its afterflow, however, calls for dismantling those structures began to be heard in Catholic centers. Vatican II designed a new Church, it was said. Some reformers were quite radical; their long-range vision involved dethroning the Church's "Holy Rulers" (Hierarchs). Unless the hierarchy's role and identity could be diminished, the changes required for total renewal in the Church system—in laws and dogma—would never come about. The anti-establishment sentiments of the 1960's helped make credible serious sorties against their leadership and the institution they personified. The times were right for denigration of hierarchy, and Vatican II clearly called the Church (and *ipso facto* the Bishop) the servant of God's people. In such circumstances early reformers in that decade found it easy to speak for those who were alienated from the Church, as it was administered up to that time. Unfortunately, the reformers showed little interest (until it was too late) in the people of faith who graced the pews every Sunday morning. Instead, they wrote and spoke almost exclusively for those who did not like existing Catholic laws, who did not believe (at least not fully) in its creeds, who wanted freedom from what they saw as oppressive religious structures, and who desired a Church which would relate to their experience as citizens of the modern world.

Also, during the 1960's, it was easy to stir audiences of the young and (oddly) members of religious communities by belittling hierarchy and priesthood, ridiculing inherited pieties, and comparing the Church to Soviet Russia. It became fashionable to assert, without having to prove it, that Sunday morning Christianity was shallow, the *Baltimore Catechism* dispensed as much "cheap truth" as the confessional dispensed "cheap grace," that obedience was unworthy of free sons and daughters of God. And among anti-intellectuals of the period, the academic elite gained fame and fortune by making personal encounter with Christ more important to real religion than convictions about doctrinal propositions.

The early success of "reformers" was surprising, because at the opening of the Council, the Church was reaping renewed respect in the secular world; its following even among the best and the brightest was enthusiastic; its converts were rushing to baptismal fonts in large numbers, precisely because the Church institution was attractive. It is something of a mystery how Catholic teachers discovered almost overnight that their students were passive Christians, guilt-ridden, victims of legalism, and socially uncaring. Battered by a host of adjectival put-downs, it was not surprising that young Catholics found it easy to dispense themselves (or be dispensed) from anything that smacked of institutionalism posing as Christ Incarnate. However, once their ties to the Church

Body were weakened or broken, the Christ of history became little more than a shadow of the one-time Self they had been trained to adore.

Later a more subtle attack on the Church followed. It took the form of X-ray studies of the Church Body conducted by academics, which allegedly showed how good the Interior Church was in comparison with the Body of the Church itself. The "bones" or the "organs" of the Church Body became "models" to be examined one by one. The end result of these studies, commonly conducted in Catholic institutions, was stress on a model (i.e., a part), not on the Church Body itself. Regard for the whole Church was diminished in favor of one of its aspects: For example, on the *Pilgrim Church,* a sinner struggling for his own salvation and evolving toward Christ's promised Kingdom in no position to make fixed demands or to provide certain guidance to its members; or on the *Servant Church* so structured, it was said, to satisfy religious needs without lording over the faithful; or on the *Herald Church,* an instrument for preaching good news, never bad; or on the *People of God Church,* a Church without an influential hierarchy; or on the *Disciple Church,* one which is always learning, rarely teaching with any certain authority.

Do these alleged models exist in practice? Students exposed to this type of indoctrination came to realize that they can find them only in what traditionally was called "the Mystical Body of Christ," in "the Sacrament necessary for salvation," that is, in "the Institutional Church." In fact, the students' faith should have made them see without having to learn all over again that the only community which could satisfy the religious needs of *their* Catholic Faith was *the* Church. This Church is, by virtue of *their* faith, the House of God and Christ's Living Presence to which they were committed. Yet, even if this reoccurred to them, teachers were not lacking who insisted again and again that the "institutional model" of the Church was unacceptable in our time, because of its nature it is collectivistic and despotic. It is not good, so the lesson went, for such a Church to dominate the gospel message. Students must search out their own gospel, with respect for the Church, of course.

The end result of indoctrination such as this was that young Catholics were sent on their way to discover a church of their liking. While the student's search continued, faith in the only Church they knew, the only Church with its hierarchy that goes back to Christ Himself, was to be replaced, not unlikely by faith in the student's privately chosen theologian.

Remarkably, this denigration of the Catholic Church goes on even to this day not only in lecture halls and classrooms of the faithful, but even in assemblies of the clergy. Undercutting the institutional Church was hardly the *aggiornamento* the Council had in mind. And if priests have become convinced that the institutional Church is less than trustworthy (many by training have become so), then authentic Catholic catechesis at the parish level becomes practically impossible. It is one thing to belong to a Church accused by her enemies of vile crimes and errors or even one treated irreverently by her own. It is another to experience on a wide scale inadequate or unfriendly theology taught to the young under Church auspices.

For good catechesis to prevail, answers to certain basic questions are called for: Is the Catholic Church the Church of Christ? Do Pope and Bishops speak for Christ with authority? When answers to these questions are given, the moment of truth has arrived. If the answers are negative or doubtful, then pronouncements by the Church on any subject are hardly binding—including the words of *Catechesi tradendae*.

These considerations apart, there is a second reason why contemporary catechesis is failing.

2. *Inculcated doubts about revelation, the Church's origins and the authenticity of Catholic teachings are a major part of the problem.*

Obviously the contemporary catechetical disorder goes beyond disobedience, bad manners, and a passing anti-establishment mood. Cardinal Oddi says that "not a few of today's attacks on the Church are going for the jugular, the very fundamentals of our Faith: the divinity of Christ, the resurrection from the dead of His true Body, our immortality, and so forth." These attacks, he said citing the Pope, are going on *within* the Church. What is at stake, therefore, is the believability of Catholicism itself. Bridges to other Christian bodies and outreach to non-believers and half-believers in Catholicism have led Catholic scholars to claim large latitude in reinterpreting the Church's doctrinal and moral norms. Alleged research discoveries, frequently in guesswork by new exegetes, are said to be the basis of a new flexibility in Catholicism. In the writings of today's widely read or well-known Catholic scholars, a Catholic can find one or the other of them asserting some or all of the following propositions, which can be found in any one of several popular biblical or theological expositions:

—No such thing as "revelation" exists if revelation means "God-out-there" once upon a time sent men to speak for Him to other men.

—The Bible, no longer to be seen as revelation in traditional terms, is to be considered instead the religious experience of a people and what they believed about God.

—Scripture is revelation in the sense of God working out nature's original endowment in an evolutionary way.

—What the Resurrection really meant is hard to say (it probably did not mean "physical resuscitation") but Jesus' followers believed He returned from the dead and made appearances.

—Christ intended to reform Judaism, not to begin a new religion.

—It was the disciples who created the separate Christian Church after they were expelled by the Synagogue establishment.

—We cannot be certain how many New Testament statements were Christ's actual words, not even the texts customarily used to prove the foundation of the Church, the primacy of Peter, apostolic succession of Bishops, the institution of the Mass as a Sacrifice and of the Priesthood, and the Sacraments.

—Christ never defined dogmas or prescribed moral codes, except to tell His followers to love God and to love and take care of each other.

—The early Church was a community of followers more than a corporate Body instituted by Jesus.

—The primitive Church took on many forms of government and adopted different, often contradictory, doctrines. Under the force of God's Spirit the Church developed in divergent ways, some of which are a distortion of or unnecessary accretions to the original Christian gospel.

—The Jews prophesied nothing, not even about a Messiah. As a persecuted people they simply verbalized their longing for a Redeemer.

—Jesus was a teacher (rabbi) in the Jewish tradition, a tradition He accepted, one in which He played a reformer's role.

—During His lifetime Jesus remained a first century Jew with the personal limitations and the superstitions of His background.

—There is a serious question whether Jesus ever considered Himself the "Son of God" except in the customary Jewish sense.

—How much Jesus knew of His "divine sonship" is a matter of some dispute.

—Jesus' knowledge of future events was inaccurate.

—His so-called prophesies and miracles are not necessarily disruptions of natural processes, but glowing post-resurrectional accounts by people who never saw Him first hand.

Various dissenting scholars raise various doubts and draw the line of belief/unbelief at different points. Only the most radical theologians subscribe to all the above propositions. But there is far more agreement on most of the items—at least on the doubts—in certain scholarly groups than those who write official documents for Pope and Bishops appreciate. There is an even larger area of agreement among dissenters on two other propositions: (1) the Church must be redefined and restructured; (2) the right of the hierarchy to define the nature of the Church or the content of its Faith must be denied or cast into serious doubt. This is what continued dissent is all about. This is why contemporary catechesis can never be truly Catholic as long as dissenters are providing the theological presuppositions which underpin the thinking of catechetical leaders.

Cardinal Oddi says the priest is "the central figure in the catechetical apostolate." Unfortunately, some priests are also the central figures in dissent and in teaching dissent to religious educators. In one major seminary, for example, an index of qualification for priestly orders is the open attitude of candidates toward "informed dissent" from official teaching! (The seminary has several dissenting faculty on staff.) On one occasion 300 catechetical leaders proceeded to give a standing ovation to a dissenting theologian who told his audience that scholars have "the right and the responsibility" to dissent from Church pronouncements they believe to be inadequate or incomplete expressions of faith. This means, of course, that the right to dissent from the magisterium which theologians claim they enjoy, catechists also enjoy. Cardinal Oddi may claim a catechist to be a man or woman given authority by the Church to teach what the Church believes. The fact is, however, that canonical teaching missions are given generally to men and women who do not teach what the Church believes. Cardinal Oddi says further that the Church needs Catechetical Institutes to prepare grass roots catechists for the parishes of the Church. The fact is that these Institutes are likely to be unacceptable among diocesan religious educators precisely because they are committed to teach what the Church believes. Even worse, such Institutes are sometimes labeled pre-Vatican II even if the only thing they are guilty of is adhering to the teaching of Vatican II.

There are still other ominous aspects to the present catechetical situation. Some priests neither know, nor care about the teacher's knowledge or positions on important Catholic doctrines, on subjects like memorization about which Pope and Bishops have already spoken affirmatively. In one Eastern parish a 14-year-old girl is teaching a first Communion class! In some parishes the priests make no effort toward sacramental preparation, orthodox or not. Some parish programs are reverse catechesis in action. Praiseworthy lay participation often involves poorly trained spokesmen for Church teaching, not the fault of the laity, surely. These sessions, which are now mandated in many places for parents of unbaptized infants, first communicants, and confirmandi, often involve debriefing parents of what they know or believe (frequently correctly) of Catholic doctrine or practice. The opening lines of the instruction not unusually claims "the Church is changing" and "Catholic teaching is not what it was when you went to school." Then, somewhere during the new catechesis, young parents may discover that baptism for their infant is not necessary, children need not confess sins, missing Mass on Sunday is no big deal, the use of contraception is a private decision, and so forth. The listeners need not be impressed by what they hear, but they must listen if their children are to receive the sacraments. Many are informed Catholics, and if they are not always the nuclear backbone of their parish, they are children of those who were. Even the dormant or half-believing Catholics in attendance, presumptively pleased by anything which might justify their laxity, know the difference between what the Bishops really teach and what they are hearing. While the compulsory exercises at the parish level are intended to be exercises in renewal or reconciliation, the evidence is scanty that any more is accomplished than the widespread reception and/or rejection of sacraments according to a new legalism, and not always a salvific one at that.

Reverse catechesis is cutting still deeper into Church order. Parish priests in some dioceses are forbidden or discouraged by their pastors from distributing communion at Sunday Mass because this (allegedly) is now the laity's role. Eucharistic ministers often are known in the parish to be contraceptive users. Religious lectors are often known anti-clericals or anti-papalists. Private confession is rarely possible. Priests tamper with the Eucharistic Prayers and other liturgical norms. And no one seems to care.

Many Bishops, including the main officers of the Vatican, have reason to question the effectiveness of catechetical instruction as it is presently conducted in the United States. Yet—what is to be done about it? Ten years of patience, workshops, and official statements ought to have convinced the Church authorities that conditions are not improving with the passage of time. Indeed, time is on the side of expanding deviance, unless remedies are administered now.

However, catechetical remedies will be useless as long as the root of the Church's teaching problem is not in religion classes at all. The source of our difficulty is in contemporary Catholic theology. Today, theologians commonly accept disagreements about the content of the Faith as a fact of life. They insinuate, if they do not declare, that such differences in Catholic teaching are legitimate or at least permissible. Church officials say no to many of these claims but religious educators take them seriously and proceed to follow the theologians rather than Bishops. At the parish level "pick and choose" Catholicism spreads among the pew holders and the private religious judgment, condemned more than once in Catholic history, prevails in the Church.

The tragedy of such faith divisions is that they ought not to have occurred at all, certainly not as a result of the Second Vatican Council. A trend toward splintering the faith unity in Catholicism was noticeable in Europe immediately after World War II. By 1950 the Holy See was aware of its dangers. Pius XII, who encouraged a renewal of Catholic scholarship two decades before Vatican II, set guidelines for theologians then which many today refuse to accept. His encyclical *Humani generis*, presently caricatured because it says that Popes can close theological discussion through official statements, is a fairly complete guidebook through the highways and byways of modern dissent. He was able to claim in 1950 that "Catholic teachers generally avoid these errors," the ones he was describing. But he was not around in 1962, when these same errors began to inundate the Church. *Humani generis* lists them all: evolutionism, existentialism, historicism, denial of natural and supernatural truth, false irenicism, trivialization of doctrine, modernism, anti-institutionalism, perversion of Sacred Scripture, rationalism, agnosticism about God, Christ and the Church, false philosophy, misuse of the positive sciences, etc. Some of Pius' statements have a prophetic ring:

> Theories that today are put forward rather covertly by some, not without cautions and distinctions, tomorrow are openly and without moderation proclaimed by others more audacious, causing scandal to many, especially among the young clergy and to the detriment of ecclesiastical authority. Though they are usually more cautious in their published works, they express themselves more openly in their writings intended for private circulation and in conferences and lectures. Moreover, these opinions are disseminated not only among members of the clergy and in seminaries and religious institutions, but also among the laity, and especially among those who are engaged in teaching youth (no. 13).

Although this description did not apply to the Church of the U.S. in 1950, it certainly applies now.

This last of the so-called "triumphal" Popes also anticipated a problem with ecclesiastical reformers who seem to consider as an obstacle to the restoration of fraternal union (i.e., of churches) things founded on the laws and the principles given by Christ and likewise on institutions founded by Him, or which are the defense and support of the integrity of the faith, and the removal of which would bring about the union of all, but only to their destruction (no. 12).

He spoke, too, of "contempt for the teaching authority of the Church itself" (no. 18), the perversion of the sense of Sacred Scripture (no. 22), the belittlement of Christianity's credibility and the Church as the Body of Christ (no. 27).

Pius XII hoped to forestall (so he said) the beginnings of these errors in the Church bodies (then confined to French and German circles) rather than "to administer the medicine after the disease has grown inveterate" (no. 40). But what he proposed as preventive medicine in 1950 has curative powers even now against a disease now chronic in American Catholicism. Here is what *Humani generis* proposed then:

41. For this reason, after mature reflection and consideration before God, that We may not be wanting in our sacred duty, We charge the Bishops and the Superiors General of Religious Orders, binding them most seriously in conscience, to take most diligent care that such opinions be not advanced in schools, in conferences or in writings of any kind, and that they be not taught in any manner whatsoever to the clergy or the faithful.

42. Let the teachers in ecclesiastical institutions be aware that they cannot with tranquil conscience exercise the office of teaching entrusted to them, unless in the instruction of their students they religiously accept and exactly observe the norms which We have ordained. That due reverence and submission which in their unceasing labor they must profess toward the teaching authority of the Church, let them instill also into the minds and hearts of their students.

Where Do We Go From Here?

Pius XII has long since gone to God but his successor once removed was lively enough in 1975 to tell French parents that their teenagers were more like the catechumens of the early centuries than the Christians of 1925. Still later John Paul II, viewing the situation well-known to Paul VI, warned catechists in 1979 about troubling young minds "with outlandish theories, useless questions, and unproductive discussions" (CT, no. 61).

Teachers competing with Popes dismiss these criticisms, preferring to explain the present Catholic malaise in political terms. If our young are uncertain about their religion, they say, it is for the reason that fundamentalists are insisting on a narrow kind of Catholicism when enlightened scholars, following the leads given in Vatican II, have already established that a fundamentalist Church has no basics in Scripture or in early Christian tradition. However, it seems farfetched to label recent Popes, who want Vatican II fully taught, as favoring fundamentalism of any kind, even when they point their pontifical fingers at the doctrinal and disciplinary errors against the Catholic Faith. At the level of catechetics one cannot continue to hear doubts being raised about Church teaching on marriage, sexuality, or the Blessed Mother, on the efficacy of Catholic sacraments, on the apostolic succession of Bishops and Pope or the infallibility of their ordinary teaching authority—and then believe that only ecclesiastical politics is involved in the repeated complaints.

The critical question of our time is more substantial: Is there an objectively True Word of God revealed by Christ and proclaimed by the Catholic Church which regularly calls for assent from professed believers?

It is one thing to speak of the Church's role to actualize by modern means the mind of Christ in the lives of those who believe in Him (1 Cor. 2:16; Phil. 2:5). It is another for today's young or old Catholic minds to be left with uncertainty by their teachers about what was in

Christ's mind in New Testament times. Or to be left in doubt whether the Church's view of Christ's mind has any relationship to God's eternal truth for them. Students or teachers by themselves certainly have no qualification to discern the truth which was revealed by Christ, even though God at every age manifests Himself to and communicates with men in private ways, sometimes miraculously as in the case of very saintly people.

What can the Church do about the misrepresentation of Catholic truth presently going on in its own institutions? Probably not much more than draw on its own two thousand years experience to counteract what is only the latest effort to substitute private religious opinion for the Word of God. This may oversimplify the serious nature of today's internal schisms, but historically the Church has responded to similar aberrations only (1) by correcting errors and (2) by teaching Catholic doctrine as effectively as it can.

John Paul II has already told Bishops that they have "the thankless task of denouncing deviations and correcting errors" (CT, no. 63). He even held up as a model for our time St. Paul's condemnation of falsehood and error (2 Tm. 4:1-5). This is a role played in recent years quite frequently by Popes. Making negative judgments and dealing with deviance and law-breaking are necessary functions of ruling—whenever such judgments are required for everybody's good.

On the other hand, it is the constant teaching of the authentic Catholic Faith, in season and out of season in the offices and institutions of the Church, which is the more important element to Church recovery of adherence by the mass of its faithful. Catholic Christianity cannot continue to appear a weak or unclear faith about things eternal or—as some would make it today—present itself as a political ideology primarily enmeshed in worldly concerns. Liberal Protestantism has tried both these approaches and its churches are empty save at concert time. George Santayana—no believer himself—saw as long ago as 1913 that in the supernatural message of the Church lays its sole dignity. The Church might always remain a voice crying in the wilderness, he said, but "it believes what it cries."

Methodologies can vary. Christ Himself spoke in folksy language, plainly in parables, even sternly. Each of the four evangelists tailored the Christ story to particular audiences. Paul—the master catechist—preached differently to the agnostics of Athens (Acts 17:23) than he did to his backsliding converts in Corinth. Even the Beloved Disciple talked differently to different churches. But means and methods are intended to enhance commitment to the Catholic Faith not submerge that very purpose of catechetics, which is personal conversion to Jesus Christ *in* His Church. And the last three words "in His Church" are an essential note of that conversion. The guiding norm for that conversion is the life experience of the Catholic Church, including the truth it is obligated to teach.

But what about the "personal experience" component and the "dialogue with life" which have been made so important for modern catechetics? Whatever their value—to given individuals in given cultural circumstances—they often lead to thinking and acting by self-proclaimed Catholics inconsistent with the life experience of the Catholic Church. Many maxims, born of latter-day existential catechetics, represent the end result of Rogerian psychological counseling more than formation in Catholic truth and virtue: "We must make our own ethical decisions"; "my conscience is infallible"; "Jesus never planned the Church as a moral arbiter"; "the Church isn't all there is to Christianity"; "spiritual maturity develops on various levels"; "mature faith is other-directed"; "prayer is sharing with others"; "the Mass isn't everything," and so forth. Great saints can find meaning in catchy phrases like these and in other maxims too. (Augustine's "Love God and do as you please" comes to mind.) But so frequently those using them today do not have reputations for sanctity and often—even as they teach the young—are known to live in defiance of Catholic definitions if these interfere with *their* personal experience of Christ.

Something else should be said about "personal experience" as an independent method of catechetics—besides its possible lack of connection with Christ or the Church. It is not really a new phenomenon in Catholic Christianity. (Instead, it is being defined differently, i.e., as a subjective and open-ended method rather than one closed around Church propositions or Church pieties.) The phrase is used so frequently nowadays that to some it appears to have risen almost out of nowhere, perhaps as the instant discovery of Vatican II. In many minds it is also equated with the new Church interest in Catholic humanism—stress on human values, personally felt faith, the kind associated with the charismatic movement, Cursillos, religious encounter sessions, programs of Renew, Search, Ministry, etc. However, faith experience—the "bolt from heaven" or the felt presence of the Holy Spirit—survived the Church long after Pentecost and has assumed many forms since then. Most religious people of every age rarely confess to such experiences, although their piety is very real. They seem to revel instead in the legends of Paul and Barnabas, Augustine and Monica, the Little Flower, Mother Seton or Mother Teresa. Yet in the parish life of modern America—long before experiential catechetics became a workshop word, good personal feeling about the Faith was commonplace—not universal, but commonplace. And it was a phenomena of the Catholic masses, not merely of an elite. This faith-experience could be observed at Eucharistic Congresses, Rosary Crusades, Parish Missions, even at the best Miraculous Medal Novenas. The Retreat Movement had it, Cana Conferences had it, so did the CFM, the Sodalities of Our Lady, the Legions of Mary. At least in the early part of the century many men who turned the Knights of Columbus, the Holy Name Societies and the Ozanam Guilds into effective apostolates were men with great feeling for the Faith. If anyone sincerely believes that faith experience waited upon existential catechetics to surface, he would have to explain the experience of those who travel hundreds of miles to see a Pope or visit the Catholic shrine at Lourdes.

Only religious myopia explains the failure to appreciate the humanity involved in the faith experience of these many millions, many of whom had never even been blessed with the nice arrangements prescribed for Catholics in the *Baltimore Catechism*. These mass Catholic phenomena were little more than the result of century-old formative procedures—including catechetics—which shepherded the faithful and the would-be-faithful around the shepherds of the Church. These movements were organized to fashion unity of faith and moral life among the faithful and represent the Church's ongoing reinforcement in Catholic lives of the truths necessary for eternal salvation.

Experiential catechetics, therefore, can be very content-filled. A good example is the catechetical formation going on among contemporary Catholic charismatic groups. If charismatics are likely to be criticized it will be for their quest of the deep religious experience, i.e., total personal conversion to Christ. Their piety is not only expressive but seeks to discern the presence of the Spirit in their lives. The charismatic movement is the religious side of the present secular drive for "self-fulfillment" and "self-expression." Even granting that some Catholic charismatics are as anti-authoritarian as the most notorious of Church dissenters, the solid core of its best known leadership subordinates personal expressiveness to the Church's criteria of religious truth and virtue, even as it continues to emphasize total personal conversion. Well known Catholic charismatics recognize the need for Catholic norms to judge the validity of their experience. Catechetical instruction of the young built on this conviction tends to be orthodox and subject to judgment by the pastors of the Church. It is this quality of personal piety and obedience to authority which has subjected charismatics to criticism for their non-involvement in socially activist causes. One conclusion should be obvious: "Experiential catechetics"—as method—has a legitimate place in religious formation as long as it leads to instruction in the Faith and morals of the Church—a necessary ingredient of any conversion to Christ which would bear the name Catholic.

But if "experiential catechetics" becomes more psychological than spiritual, if its open-endedness is used to make independence of Church authority a norm of Catholic life, if private experience means something different than Catholic formation, if involvement in socio-political causes is made out to be a substitute for personal holiness or obedience to the Church, then we are talking about a catechetical course leading to liberal Protestantism or Secular Christianity more than a road to Rome.

Who is going to see to it that young Catholics are taught what it means to be a good Catholic? Cardinal Oddi informs us that the Holy See now has ready for publication a universal outline of Catholic doctrine to guide Bishops (in the words of *Catechesi tradendae*, no. 30) to "prepare genuine catechisms which will be faithful to the essential content of revelation." Such an outline can help but only if Pius XII's counsel in *Humani generis* takes hold of the contemporary Church: (1) Bishops must take care of their own institutions; (2) Teachers must in conscience reverence the teaching authority of the Church and instill that reverence in the minds and hearts of their students.

If these two conditions are not met, Johnny and Jackie Young Catholic will never know what it means to be a young Catholic.

CHAPTER SEVEN

Contemporary Catechesis in the United States: State of the Question

Rev. Msgr. George A. Kelly

Catholics, having heard all the complaints, may well be getting tired of hearing the word "catechetics." If that is so, the reason may be that no area of pastoral ministry is still so unsettled as that of teaching the Catholic Faith in the post-Vatican II Church.

The continuing concern of Church authorities about "catechetics" is manifest in the many official documents that have emanated from various Bishops' offices since the close of the Council. Beginning with the *General Catechetical Directory* of 1971 which Rome hoped would reverse the tide of doctrineless catechetics, there followed a series of other official documents which were content oriented, especially the U.S. Bishops' Pastoral *To Teach as Jesus Did* (1972) and their *Basic Teachings for Catholic Religious Education* (1973). When the catechetical world continued to be unsettled—i.e., Catholic programs were not uniformly teaching precisely what Catholic authorities wanted taught—Paul VI convoked the Synod of Bishops (1977). The purpose here was to regularize catechetics once and for all. (Paul VI postponed discussion of the family in order to take up first evangelization [1974] and then catechesis of the faithful.) This 1977 Synod was hardly underway when the American hierarchy undertook consultations which resulted in the publication of its own *National Catechetical Directory*

(1979). Shortly thereafter (October 16, 1979), only days after his return from what he called his catechetical journey to the U.S., John Paul II issued *Catechesi tradendae,* the exhortation designed to motivate catechists, especially the clergy, to conduct the catechetical enterprise according to the mind of the Church.

Catechesi tradendae, planned as a new charter for teaching Christ to contemporary Catholics, called for modern catechists to expound "revelation as transmitted by the universal magisterium of the Church in its solemn or ordinary form" (no. 7).

One of the reasons for the convocation of the 1977 Synod of Bishops was the failure since 1965 to transmit revelation in this way. The Bishops looked to Paul VI to provide leadership for catechists. He died. John Paul I died. So it was left for the present Pope to articulate the Church's Faith anew—the Faith that was to be transmitted creatively and authentically, especially by Bishops and priests.

Even so, many religious educators pay little heed to what comes from Rome on catechetical matters. Within the past year, for example, 300 catechetical leaders gave a standing ovation to a dissenting theologian who told them that theologians have both "the right and the responsibility" to dissent from Church pronouncements they believe to be inadequate or incomplete expressions of the Faith.

This is the background of the visit by Silvio Cardinal Oddi to the United States in May 1981. The Prefect of the Holy See's Congregation of the Clergy came to celebrate the second anniversary of *Catechesi tradendae* and to reaffirm its message. As the Church's chief catechist, under the Pope, Cardinal Oddi's visit had an official purpose—to expound the policy of the Church contained in *Catechesi tradendae.* It was clear that this prefect for the world's Catholic clergy was conversant with the catechetical situation in the U.S., one not dissimilar from conditions in Western Europe. William McCready's data, presented to the 1981 NCEA convention, were known to him, and he was not surprised by the information gathered for the New York Symposium by Brooklyn's Bishop Bevilacqua. What interested Cardinal Oddi, however, was the future of catechetics, not its recent past. He spoke of the importance of proper training for new catechists, of authentic teaching in diocesan and university programs, and of the central role of priests in catechesis. He went out of his way more than once to explain why catechetics came under the jurisdiction of the *Congregation of the Clergy*. Because, he said, catechetics is not an educational enterprise but a pastoral apostolate. The chief responsibility for its exercise falls on clergy, especially on Bishops.

Cardinal Oddi was particularly hopeful that properly managed Catechetical Institutes working closely with Bishops and with his office would ameliorate some of the more troublesome difficulties faced by the Church in this critical area of evangelization.

However, the more important aspects of the visit (beyond what he had to say) may be the *nature of the audience who came to hear him* and *the nature of what the people said to him*. The occasion was a symposium at St. John's University (NYC) publicized as a meeting on "Pope John Paul II—Catechist" in recognition of a volume bearing that name published the same month by the *Franciscan Herald Press*. Cardinal Cooke wrote the foreword to this commentary on *Catechesi tradendae* by Fr. Robert Levis and Fr. Michael Wrenn. Simultaneously the *Daughters of St. Paul* published a commentary entitled *"Going, Teach..."*. Assembling priests, educators, and parents to hear what Rome was saying about catechesis two years after John Paul II had set down universal guidelines for the Church seemed an appropriate thing to do.

When the SJU program was developed every Bishop received an invitation to participate, as did important superiors of religious communities, religious educators, and all pastors, principals, and parents groups in the New York metropolitan area. Cardinal Oddi's visit was taken in some quarters as a hopeful sign of a resurgence of interest in authentic catechesis and the beginning of an end to deviance from Church policy and Catholic doctrine. In other places fear was expressed that the coming of a Vatican representative was itself negative criticism of the American Catholic performance in catechetical renewal.

Several scores of Bishops sent encouraging letters, a few arranged to attend or send representatives, nationally known and nationally based catechetical leaders traveled from Canada, Washington, California, New England and the South to hear the Roman Cardinal. The actual participants, 300 in number, represented a cross-section of religious educators in the United States. Half of the priests in attendance, half of the religious, and one-quarter of the laity came from regions beyond the New York metropolitan area. Although most of the religious were members of communities generally in conformity with Vatican regulations, members of religious communities in a posture of defiance toward Rome were well represented. Most lay people in attendance were local teachers or parents. Organizations, such as *Catholics United for the Faith* and several family associations, sent members of their administrative staff. Half of the priests were parish clergy, the other half were teachers. Seminary and university professors manifested a significant interest in the Symposium. Noticeably absent, however, were diocesan education officers who by reason of geography would, one might expect, wish to hear the latest from Rome on what obviously is a particular challenge to the Church in the U.S. While the excuses for non-attendance were plausible, it was also clear that some of those making them were already moving their dioceses in directions at variance with the intentions and decrees of the Holy See.

The two-day discussion between the Bishops and the audience was serious at times, occasionally exhilarating, and, due to Cardinal Oddi's extraordinary sense of humor, was frequently funny. The interchange between participants and speakers can be summarized under five headings: *facts, teaching, textbooks, professional experts,* and *clergy.*

Few at the Symposium seemed pleased with the *factual situation* of present-day catechesis, not even the Bishops present. Religious instruction in earlier days never resulted in 100 percent believers or performing Catholics, but the latest reports that Catholic school children hardly merited more than a passing grade for what they knew about the Faith was hardly encouraging. Compared to earlier generations, failures in present day faith-commitment were marked. Of particular concern to parents was the deviance of their young from Catholic sexual norms.

One nationally known religious educator rose to ask a Bishop—"Are we really teaching the Faith?" He was mindful of what was referred to in many classrooms as official Church teaching, but of the doubts, too, of certain members of the catechetical establishment about Christ, eternal life, the Church, and the reception of the sacraments. Unbelief, he said, was not rare in earlier generations of alleged Catholics, but now is being presented under diocesan auspices. A Bishop responding to the priest in question expressed sympathy with the concern, especially because he had read that a well-known Catholic educator had said that religious dissent among the young is a healthy sign. The Bishop did not think that Christ had come to confuse His own no more than He could call successful any catechesis that led listeners away from Catholic norms.

Blame for the present catechetical difficulties was placed partly on *teachers*, partly on *textbooks* mandated or approved for religion classes. One question was asked several times: Does anyone inquire into the faith commitment of the teachers themselves? Professionally certified teachers are important, but more essential is their full commitment to the Church for whom they work. Teachers today who positively promote religious error are not uncommon in today's classes. A large number leave large gaps of doctrine and morality uncovered or unexplained. "Is a bad religion teacher ever removed from his post as a bad mathematician might be?"—another parent asked. The teacher, as the surrogate for the parents and for the Church, is a force for good or evil depending on how he or she exemplifies the holiness of Christ and the Church or how either fails in the role.

The *textbook* situation, as seen by the Symposium participants, was also a matter of controversy. Part of the reason was that Catholic textbook authors rely more on professional "expert" opinion than on Church documents, especially on the opinion of experimental psychologists. Psychologists are mostly men of good will and are competent in the use of the tools of their trade, but they are hardly the last word on religious education or moral training of Christians. First, because, as Professor Paul Vitz indicated, experimental psychology has been cut off from religion and philosophy for more than a century, thus rendering its conclusions tentative as to alleged "facts" and perilous as to "theories," if applied to religious and moral training. Secondly, because secular theories of moral development and values clarification no longer are considered satisfactory by *secular scholars* nor as competent models of moral training. In spite of these reservations, secular psychology has dominated Catholic textbooks and diocesan workshops for more than a decade. Catholic teachers now follow, as the textbooks indicate, psychological theories more than their own educational tradition. As pedagogical practice encourages Catholic teachers to stress the goodness in their students, practicing psychologists (to be distinguished from experimentalists and laboratory technicians) are beginning to acknowledge the evil in man and his disposition to evil. Contrariwise, the Catholic education establishment today operates out of what is only a recent legacy, viz., man's untainted goodness will fructify if natural processes of growth are allowed to develop. As a result they have tended to eschew indoctrination, especially about God's law and sin, memory training and discipline, the very stuff of education which secular educators are seeking to recapture. A major point made at the SJU Symposium was this: Whatever else can be said of experimental psychology, it is clear that some experts at least, especially those with Catholic Faith, are beginning to agree with parents that you cannot build a Church on incompetent secular values or techniques.

One other aspect of the textbook question and the professional experts who dominate their composition is related to the book business itself. Catechetical book publishing is big business, often involving firms owned and managed by conglomerates far removed from religion or its concerns. After Vatican II these firms came to dominate, as never before, the make-up and content of religion books. Newness and change, even revolution, were popular during the 1960's and profitable. Tradition, orthodoxy, even sectarianism, hitherto a guarantee of sales success, became money losers, except among evangelical Protestants who published their own tracts and textbooks. Taking over the writing of religion books, secular publishing houses paid handsome royalties to willing collaborators and adopted a publishing format which paid handsome dividends. Since the captured audiences were counted in the millions, it is not difficult to see that monetary returns involved were high. The catechisms once known by the name of their priest authors were big sellers no more and they suffered by comparison because they lacked pictures, pictographs, and jazzy color schemes. Imprecisions or lacunae in doctrinal content in new books was overlooked because post-Vatican II was considered a time of experimentation. In spite of a long list of official statements seeking to restore a proper balance between good pedagogy and sound doctrine, years passed before the experimental texts were amended.

What was also disturbing to some educators and parents—over and above the shortcomings of the popular texts—was the successful effort in many dioceses, sometimes with episcopal approval, to discourage or ban absolutely the use of so-called "orthodox" texts, even after the publishers of these books went to great length to modernize their style and composition. One theologian at the St. John's Symposium went so far as to assert that diocesan education offices exceeded their authority in censoring books, since Bishops could not delegate such authority to educators as such. He also maintained that pastors had rights of their own to determine what was necessary for the religious education of their parish children and that offended pastors, religious, or publishers had a right (if the content of the Catholic Faith was the issue) to use the due process machinery of the diocese against the educators who insist on limiting their pastors' rights in the religious formation of their own young. At one point in the discussion Cardinal Oddi intervened to request that offended parties feel free to communicate their grievances to him. Negative sanctions against authentic textbooks (sometimes on the ground that they represent the Church of Trent rather than the Church of Vatican II) and the studied harassment of teachers who favor them, has been particularly oppressive whenever a local Bishop becomes personally involved in the conflict. Religious communities of nuns have departed or have been forced out of schools in dioceses over books that are solidly Catholic, are acceptable elsewhere, some which even have the approval of the highest officers of the Church.

This explains why, according to Cardinal Oddi, the *Congregation of the Clergy* in Rome has in preparation a universal catechetical handbook which will contain the basic teachings of the Church to be included in the catechisms or catechetical directories of all hierarchies. *Catechesi tradendae* encourages national conferences of Bishops to elaborate catechisms which meet the particular needs of special populations with distinctive cultures. Nonetheless, Rome has discovered—beginning with the Dutch Catechism in 1967—that national catechisms are frequently defective in their treatment of important Catholic doctrines such as original sin or the virginity of Mary. These imprecisions were once justified on the ground that some account should be taken of the theological disputes currently raging in the Church. The Holy See thinks differently—that theorizing has no place in basic catechisms. In this, Rome is supported by believing parents and children who manifest enthusiasm for full and honest treatment of those supernatural Christian truths which the intellectual elite tend to downplay.

Catechesi tradendae insisted too that, in spite of its ecumenical dimension, catechesis involves teaching "the fullness of revealed truths and of the means of salvation instituted by Christ" and "found in the Catholic Church" (no. 32). John Paul II in the same exhortation went so far as to single out for praise Paul VI's "Creed of the People of God" for its summary of "the essential elements of the Catholic Faith, especially those that presented greater difficulty or risked being ignored" (no. 28). Indeed, the present Pope made Catholic creeds the "sure point of reference for the content of catechesis."

At the St. John's Symposium, a great deal of discussion revolved around Bishops and priests upon whom Cardinal Oddi (following *Catechesi tradendae*, nos. 63-64) placed major responsibility for catechesis.

A final word ought to be said about the overall tone of the SJU Symposium on catechetics and Cardinal Oddi's participation. The scholarly presentations were all thoughtful and constructive even though realistic about the American Catholic scene. Bishops Bevilacqua and Vaughan, no less than Professor Vitz, Sister Michele and Sister Catherine were by training and experience intellectually competent witnesses of the areas of catechesis they were asked to address. Cardinal Oddi sat beside his brother Bishops in a spirit of good fellowship which spilled over to the audience. Because the audience was small enough to encourage wide-scale participation, most of the discussion was sensible. The general outcome was renewed enthusiasm for the Faith among the participants and for the work of catechetical instruction. The involvement of Cardinal Oddi and East Coast Bishops helped generate the positive results.

The issue most often raised was the continued presence in catechesis and in catechetical training of teachers who openly or subtly undermine Catholic teaching or inculcate distrust of the Church hierarchy. Even in this touchy area the discussion was reasonable, except for those testy characters who manage to be truculent at all conventions. Unlike colloquia at some other meetings, the negative questions at SJU were aimed at supporting the Magisterium, not tearing it down or explaining it away.

Mother Angelica, founder of Eternal Word Network, once was asked about the editorial policy of her pioneering effort in Catholic cable television. She indicated in reply that she intended to expound and promote the Faith of the Catholic Church. When pressed further on her openness to dissenting Catholic opinions she continued: "Is being orthodox all that much of a crime these days?" She gathered the impression that in certain Catholic quarters it is. Unfortunately, the word "orthodoxy" is often associated with "right-wing" Catholicism. Surely, if catechesis is discussed in political terms there can be found "right-wing" Catholics who reject the authority of the Church in certain doctrinal areas (e.g., the Lefebvreites), others who cannot abide the social teaching of the Church and some who are unhappy with the hierarchy's implementation of legitimate decrees from Vatican II. One cannot dismiss either Catholics who yearn for the old days and the old ways or who persist in defending traditions or appearances which Church hierarchy have already changed. There are also to be found Catholics who sincerely believe that the strictest theological or disciplinary position is the most Christian. Theologians once called these people tutiorists or absolute tutiorists. When totalled together these anti-renewal groups may comprise significant numbers. But it is virtually impossible to assert whether there are more "right-wing" extremists in the contemporary Church than "left-wingers," i.e., those who (like Lefebvreites) deny doctrines they do not accept or who cede to the faithful a large area of freedom to decide how little Catholic doctrine or norms they need accept without abandoning Catholic identity. Given the cultural mood of the modern moment, "left wing" is more respectable today than "right wing." It is probably true to say that in the United States at least the more frequent denials of the right of Church authority on behalf of Catholic truth to bind minds or conscience comes from the quarter of the Church fashionably called "left of center" or "progressive."

There are still large bodies of Catholics, however, who are not politically "right," (and because of their social commitments often meet the standards set for left wing affiliation), who are legitimately concerned about the violence being done to the meaning of Christ's revelation and of the Catholic Faith in particular. Variously commentators speak of a "crisis of faith" or a "crisis of authority," depending on where one places the locus of the Church difficulty. No matter how it is described, whether in theological or political terms, the crisis can be alleviated only by important agreements and decisions which must be seen as binding. Uncontrolled divisions, if unduly prolonged, must of necessity lead to internal schism. Interventions by prelates like Cardinal Oddi are helpful supports to those who believe that the last word on doctrine belongs to the voice of Rome.

John Paul II closed *Catechesi tradendae* with the reminder that we are all bound to the universal mission of the Church given by Christ: "Go and make disciples of all nations." If this means anything at all it means one faith under one Christ with the limits of pluralism determined by one hierarchy under one Pope.

Index of Names and Subjects

Adult Education, 65, 79, 150ff.
American Church, 14-16
Atheism in Kohlberg, 119

Baltimore Catechism, 185, 212
Banning Textbooks, 221
Baptism, 79-80
Basic Teachings, 194, 214
Bevilacqua, Bishop Anthony, 37ff., 216
Brooklyn Dioceses, 38ff.

Catechesi Tradendae, 13, 16-18, 23, 26, 30, 34, 37, 69, 76, 123, 155, 166, 176, 195, 213ff.
Catechesis
—and adults, 150ff.
—and hierarchy, 180ff.
—and priests, 22
—and theology, 160ff.
—competence, 33
—content, 78
—fidelity, 29
—liturgy, 71ff.
—of old and young, 26-27
—pastoral achievements, 62ff.
—pastoral problems, 53ff., 157, 183, 208
—pastoral view, 37-88
Catechists, 19-20, 24, 28
Catechizing the Poor, 138ff.
Catholic Problem, 186ff.
Catholic Schools, 15
Catholicity of Youth, 39ff.
Catholics United for the Faith, 217
Christian Moral Development, 120ff.
Christian Response to Values Clarification, 100ff.
Church, Catholic, 23, 196
Commandments, 131ff.
Confraternity of Christian Doctrine, 16, 35-48, 64, 161ff., 183
Confusion, 183
Congregation of the Clergy, 13, 16
Contradictory Pluralism, 173
Coordinators, Religious, 66
Creeds, Catholic, 193ff.

Credo of the People of God, (Paul VI), 193

Daughters of St. Paul, 216
De Catechezandis Rudibus, 185
Development of Doctrine, 170ff.
Developmental Theories, 101ff. 179ff.
Dewey, John, 89, 101ff.
Disbelief, Growing, 197ff.
Doctrine, Catholic, 24, 70ff., 156ff., 169ff.
Doctrinal Method, 194
Dutch Catechism, 221

Ecumenism, 24
Empirical Critique of Kohlberg, 105ff.
Experiential Catechetics, 189ff., 210ff.

Faith, attacks on, 19, 70ff., 156ff., 197ff., 208
Faith of Our Fathers, 185
Faithful, Catholic, 20
Freedom, Religious, 24

General Catechetical Directory, 38, 193, 214
Gilligan, Carol, 116ff.
"Going, Teach..." 216
Gurrieri, Fr. John, 73

Hierarchical Church, 23, 180
Hispanic Catholics, 138ff.
Hogan, Robert, 108ff.
Home Catechesis, 204
Humanae Vitae, 177
Humani Generis, 206ff.

Kelly, Msgr. George A., 36, 185ff.
Kingdom of God, 32
Kohlberg, Lawrence, 101ff.

Lay Catechists, 14, 204
Levis, Fr. Robert, 216
Liturgy and Catechesis, 72ff.

Magisterium, 31, 70ff., 76, 157, 164ff., 180
McCready, William, 42ff., 215
McKeon, Sr. Michelle, 138ff.
Methodologies, 210
Mother Angelica, 223
Mother Teresa, 142
Mysterium Fidei (Paul VI), 173

National Catechetical Directory, 16, 34, 38, 72, 75, 132, 151, 194, 214
National Opinion Research Center, 42

Oddi, Silvio Cardinal, 13ff., 196ff., 203, 215ff.
O'Hara, Bishop Edwin V., 16

Parent Participation, 78
Pastoral Achievements, 62ff.
Pastoral Problems, 53ff.
Pastors, 26
Penance and Reconciliation, 80, 179
Piaget, Jean, 101ff.
Pluralism, 23, 169ff.
Politics, 33
Pope John Paul I, 25
Pope John Paul II, 19, 21-22, 123, 150ff., 166, 175, 195, 209ff.
Pope Paul VI, 38, 171
Pope Pius XII, 123, 206ff.
Power, Fr. David, 75
Prayer, 129
Priest Teachers, 197ff.
Psychological Development, 101ff., 179ff.

Raths, Louis, 89ff.

Recommendations, 75ff.
Rejection of Church as Teacher, 70ff.
Relevance and Catechesis, 175ff.
Religious Educators, 187ff.
Religious Knowledge Survey, 45ff.
Religious Teachers, 198ff., 218
Revelation, 30, 124, 164ff., 200ff., 215
Reverse Catechesis, 205ff.
Rockville Centre Diocese, 150
Rouet, Albert, 73

Shea, Sr. Theresa Catherine, 150ff.
Signs of the Times, 30, 31
Simon, Sidney, 89ff.
South Bronx, 138ff.
St. John's University, 13, 216ff.
St. Thomas Aquinas, 170ff.
State of the Question, 214ff.
Statistics, Religious, 39ff.
Synod of Bishops, 122, 214

Teaching the Faith, 218
Textbooks, Catechetical, 218ff.
Theology and Catechesis, 160ff.
Truth, Catholic, 23, 156ff., 164ff.

Values Clarification, 89ff., 122-123
Vatican II, 22, 32, 76, 153, 161, 193, 198
Vaughan, Bishop Austin, 160ff.
Vincentian Fathers, 13
Vitz, Paul, 89ff.

Wolterstorff, Nicholas, 93, 111ff.
Wrenn, Fr. Michael, 216
Wright, John Cardinal, 15

Other Titles in This Series

Catholic Ministries in Our Time
Edited by George A. Kelly

Distinctions between the ministerial priesthood of the ordained and the common priesthood of the faithful. 158 pages
cloth $4.00; paper $3.00 — RA0035

Human Sexuality in Our Time—What the Church Teaches
Edited by George A. Kelly

Noted educators treat such timely topics as sex and sanctity, contraception, biblical thoughts on human sexuality, morality and sexuality, catechesis and sexuality, and Church teaching on marriage.
cloth $4.00; paper $3.00 — RA0115

The Sacrament of the Eucharist in Our Time
Edited by George A. Kelly

A compact theology of the Eucharist by the faculty of the Institute for Advanced Studies in Catholic Doctrine at St. John's University.

Aspects treated include the Eucharist in Catholic Tradition; The Eucharist as a Sacrifice; Old and New Conceptions; Christ in the Eucharist; Presence and Reality; Discerning the Body of the Lord; Who May Receive the Eucharist; The Eucharist in Catechesis—Current Approaches.
108 pages
cloth $3.75; paper $2.25 — RA0155

The Sacrament of Penance in Our Time
Edited by George A. Kelly

In-depth lectures on the sacrament of Reconciliation covering such topics as: Socio-historical questions about the penitential discipline of the Catholic Church; Penance and the Second Vatican Council; The New Rite of Penance; Penance as renewal and reconciliation, etc. Contributors to this timely book are Robert I. Bradley, S.J., Bruce A. Williams, O.P., Joseph E. Hogan, C.M., Eugene Kevane, John A. Hardon, S.J. 165 pages
cloth $4.00 — RA0160

The Teaching Church in Our Time
Edited by George A. Kelly

Covers the relationship to the magisterium of Catholic doctrine in the following areas—Scripture, Tradition, modernism, infallibility, catechetics and sexual matters. The contributors are Msgr. Eugene Kevane; Fr. Manuel Miguens, OFM; Fr. Robert Bradley, SJ; Fr. John Hardon, SJ; Fr. Joseph Hogan, CM; Fr. Bruce A. Williams, OP; all faculty members for the Institute for Advanced Studies in Catholic Doctrine at St. John's University, New York City. 250 pages
cloth $6.00; paper $4.50 — RA0190

VATICAN II AND POST-CONCILIAR DOCUMENTS

The 16 Documents of Vatican II

The paperback and plastic edition includes a topical index and commentaries from outstanding Council Fathers. 760 pages cloth or plastic $6.95; paper $3.25 — EP1010

In Pamphlet Form:

Constitution on the Sacred Liturgy (Sacrosunctum concilium) 25¢ — EP0250Z

Decree on the Media of Social Communication (Inter mirifica) 15¢ — EP0380Z

Dogmatic Constitution on the Church (Lumen gentium) 50¢ — EP0460Z

Decree on Ecumenism (Unitatis redingratio) 25¢ — EP0330Z

Decree on the Catholic Churches of the Eastern Rite (Orientalium Ecclesiarum) 15¢ — EP0370Z

Declaration on Christian Education (Gravissimum educationis) 15¢ — EP0280Z

Declaration on the Relation of the Church to Non-Christian Religions (Nostra aetate) 10¢ — EP0300Z

Decree Concerning the Pastoral Office of Bishops in the Church (Christus Dominus) 30¢ — EP0320Z

Decree on the Adaptation and Renewal of Religious Life (Perfectae caritatis) 15¢ — EP0350Z

Decree on Priestly Training (Optatam totius) 15¢ — EP0340Z

Decree on the Apostolate of the Laity (Apostolicam actuositatem) 30¢ — EP0360Z

Dogmatic Constitution on Divine Revelation (Dei Verbum) 25¢ — EP0450Z

Declaration on Religious Freedom (Dignitatis humanae) 20¢ — EP0290Z

Decree on the Ministry and Life of Priests (Presbyterorum ordinis) 30¢ — EP0390Z

Decree on the Mission Activity of the Church (Ad gentes) 30¢ — EP0400Z

Pastoral Constitution on the Church in the Modern World (Gaudium et spes) 65¢ — EP0910Z

Documents Implementing Vatican II

Apostolic Constitution on Fast and Abstinence (Poenitemini) 10¢ — EP0030Z

Apostolic Constitution on Indulgences (Indulgentiarum doctrina) 20¢ — EP0040Z

Apostolic Constitution on New Roman Missal (Missale romanum). And: **Motu Proprio on Liturgical Year and New Universal Roman Calendar** (Paschalis mysterii) 20¢ — EP0050Z

Apostolic Constitution on the Post-Council Jubilee 10¢ — EP0060Z

Apostolic Constitution on the Sacrament of the Anointing of the Sick 10¢ — EP0070Z

Apostolic Exhortation on the Renewal of the Religious Life According to the Teaching of the Second Vatican Council (Evangelica testificatio) 25¢ — EP0090Z

Apostolic Letter Determining Norms for Expediting Marriage Cases 10¢ — EP0110Z

Apostolic Letter Ecclesiae sanctae 35¢ — EP0120Z

Apostolic Letter on Mixed Marriages (Matrimonia mixta). And: **Statement of U.S. Bishops on the implementation of the Apostolic Letter on Mixed Marriages** 25¢ — EP0130Z

Apostolic Letter Regarding the Sacred Order of the Diaconate and an Apostolic Letter by which the Discipline of First Tonsure, Minor Orders and Subdiaconate in the Latin Church Is Reformed (August, 1972) 15¢ — EP0140Z

Basic Scheme for Priestly Training (Ratio fundamentalis institutionis sacerdotalis) 50¢ — EP0170Z

Council Closing Speeches 30¢ — EP0260Z

Declaration Regarding the Safeguarding of Faith in the Mysteries of the Incarnation and of the Most Blessed Trinity from Some Recent Errors 10¢ — EP0310Z

Directory on Ecumenism 15¢ — EP0430Z

General Norms for Restoring the Permanent Diaconate in the Latin Church (Sacrum diaconatus ordinem) 15¢ — EP0510Z

In Defense of the Catholic Doctrine on the Church (Mysterium Ecclesiarum) 25¢ — EP0590Z

Instruction Concerning Cases When Other Christians Can Be Admitted to Eucharistic Communion in the Catholic Church 15¢ — EP0600Z

Instruction on Contemplative Life and on the Enclosure of Nuns (Venite seorsum) 25¢ — EP0610Z

Instruction on the Liturgy (Inter oecumenici) 25¢ — EP0660Z

Instruction on Mixed Marriages (Matrimonii sacramentum) 15¢ — EP0620Z

Instruction on Music in the Liturgy (Musicam sacram) 20¢ — EP0630Z

Instruction on the Renewal of Religious Formation (Renovationis causam) 25¢ — EP0640Z

Instruction on Sacramental Communion in Particular Circumstances (Immensae caritatis) 10¢ — EP0650Z

Instruction on Worship of the Eucharistic Mystery (Eucharisticum mysterium) 25¢ — EP0670Z

Motu Proprio Sacram liturgiam 15¢ — EP0790Z

Pastoral Instruction for the Application of the Decree of the Second Vatican Ecumenical Council on the Means of Social Communication (Communio et progressio) 50¢ — EP0920Z

Pastoral Norms Concerning the Administration of General Sacramental Absolution 10¢ — EP0930Z

Second Instruction on the Liturgy (Tres abhinc annos) 15¢ — EP0990Z

Synodal Document on Justice in the World 15¢ — EP0680Z

Synodal Document on the Ministerial Priesthood 25¢ — EP0750Z

Third Instruction of the Correct Application of the Constitution on the Sacred Liturgy 15¢ — EP1050Z

Toward the Meeting of Religions—Suggestions for Dialogue 35¢ — EP1080Z

Documents on Catechesis

Apostolic Exhortation on Catechesis in Our Time (Catechesi Tradendae)
Pope John Paul II
   The Holy Father's guidelines for handing on the Faith today. Given on Oct. 16, 1979. 68 pages 60¢ — EP0185

Letter to All Bishops of the Church and to All Priests of the Church
Pope John Paul II
   Issued on Holy Thursday, 1979. 34 pages; 25¢ — EP0688

On Evangelization in the Modern World (Evangelii Nuntiandi)
Pope Paul VI
   Issued on December 8, 1975. 64 pages; 40¢ — EP0850

On the Teaching of Christian Doctrine (Acerbo Nimis)
Pope Pius X
16 pages; 20¢ — EP0145

Catechetics

Basic Catechism
Daughters of St. Paul
   This concise, direct book presents the fundamentals of the Catholic Faith in a question-and-answer format with related scriptural quotations.

Thoroughly indexed for ready reference, it is a vital handbook for anyone desiring to deepen or clarify his belief. 208 pages
cloth $3.00; paper $1.50 — RA0007

"Going, Teach..."
—Commentary on the Apostolic Exhortation *Catechesi Tradendae* of Pope John Paul II

Coordinator: Cesare Bonivento, PIME
Edited by the Institute of Missionary Catechesis
Translated by the Daughters of St. Paul

In more than 600 pages, 40 specialists, representing many nations, give a commentary on the Apostolic Exhortation of Pope John Paul II on Catechesis in Our Time.

On the eve of the 21st century, His Holiness re-echoes Christ's command: "Going, teach all nations..." (Mt. 28:19). Every believer to a certain degree is responsible for catechesis, for handing on the faith he has received as a gift—handing it on in its beauty and in its totality. The Church, "the great giver as well as the great receiver of catechesis," presents Christ the Teacher to everyone —to children, adolescents and adults.

Contains the complete text of *Catechesi Tradendae*, and an index of the commentary. 728 pages
cloth $19.95 — RA0114

Media Impact and You
Daughters of St. Paul

Designed to capture the casual reader and student alike, this concise book strives to impress youth with media's power to influence the way people think, speak and act. Thus, the necessity of media formation. As a text, the book can be the basis of a semester media course. Indexed.
128 pages
cloth $2.95; paper $1.95 — CA0185

One Family Under God
Principles laid down by Vatican II, recent Popes and the American Bishops for fashioning a world more according to man's dignity. Provides guidelines for an authentic search for true brotherhood. cloth $3.00; paper $2.00 — CA0180

Who Is Jesus?
Probes the Divine Master's life, step by practical step. Light is thrown on youth's authentic search for a real Messiah; on everyone's desire for true liberation; on Eucharistic Communion with most profound repercussions. Confusing ideas about Jesus' identity are carefully sifted and our own identity in relation to His emerges in sharp relief. Compiled from the talks of Pope Paul VI. paper $2.25 — CA0190

Religion for Adults
Answers to Your Questions
Rev. Richard V. Lawlor, SJ

A competent theologian answers some of the most crucial questions of our day, touching on such topics as marriage and family life, doctrine and morals, the Bible, prayer, etc. 222 pages
cloth $5.00; paper $4.00 — RA0005

A Brief Summary of the Ten Commandments
Daughters of St. Paul
A theological question and answer treatment. Complete with scriptural facts and Vatican II pastoral teachings. 96 pages
Magister paperback $1.25 — CA0200

Catechism for Adults
Rev. James Alberione, SSP, STD
Theology at your fingertips. This volume clearly and concisely offers answers to the questions the man of today is asking. Ideal for individual reading, convert instruction classes, and discussion groups. 272 pages
Magister paperback $2.25 — RA0010

The Catholic Church Through the Ages
Rev. Martin P. Harney, SJ
Thorough and factual. The author, historian and long-time Church history professor, treats every major issue from the era of primitive Christianity up into our own twentieth century. His style reveals his familiarity with the events he relates. Ideal as reference material, this newest work could also lend itself very well to classroom use. 600 pages
cloth $12.00; paper $11.00 — RA0030

The Christ of Vatican II
Compiled by the Daughters of St. Paul
To a world that has in a sense lost a consciousness of things divine, and where a "death of God" theology is in vogue, the Second Vatican Council presents a vivid and vibrant profile of Christ the Lord. 80 pages
cloth $2.00; paper $1.00 — RA0040

Christ the Answer
Rev. Peter Sullivan
Appealingly-presented apologetics stressing the implication of the divinity of Christ for the modern world. "Valuable reading for the layman or the person involved in CCD work." Rev. Anton Wambach 272 pages
Magister paperback $1.95 — RA0050

Christianity and Politics
Rev. James V. Schall, S.J.
Covers such subjects as the effect of Christian thought on politics, atheism and politics, Christianity and the "cures" of poverty, and America in recent Catholic social thought. 336 pages
cloth $6.95; paper $5.95 — MS0123

Christianity in the Twentieth Century
John A. Hardon, SJ
An in-depth examination of the major issues and ideas that are shaping the development of Catholic, Protestant and Orthodox Christianity in our modern "age of communications." A book of realism and hope. 528 pages
cloth $5.95; paper $2.95 — RA0070

The Church: Life-Giving Union With Christ
John Cardinal Krol
To all who are interested in knowing the mystery of the Catholic Church today, His Eminence gives answers in language which is striking and vigorous. Beginning with the implications of the Second Vatican Council, he leads his readers to look toward a future filled with hope. 682 pages
cloth $7.50; paper $5.95 — RA0055

The Church's Amazing Story
Daughters of St. Paul
   Concise and up-to-date, this volume offers an objective, balanced view of the Church in every age, highlighting outstanding events and personalities in a vivid, honest manner. Another feature—continuity without extraneous dates and material. And because many profit greatly by viewing the happenings of today in the light of history, notes are provided at chapter endings to personalize and spiritualize the lessons of yesterday for the reader on the current scene. 312 pages
cloth $6.00; paper $5.00 — CA0100

The Eternal Wisdom
Rev. James Alberione, SSP, STD
   Often called a one book encyclopedia of the Catholic faith—a brilliant four-color art master accompanies each page of explanation with Scripture references throughout. An ideal family book and convert manual. 180 pages
cloth $7.00 — RA0090

The Faith We Live By
Daughters of St. Paul
   One of the magnificent legacies left us by Pope Paul—his Credo of the People of God, entirely explained in these pages. A tremendous background source on the Catholic faith steeped in Scripture, quotations from the Fathers of the Church and Vatican II documents—poems, prayers, photos!· 400 pages
cloth $7.00; paper $6.00 — CA0110

General Moral Theology
Most Rev. Antonio Lanza and Most Rev. Pietro Palazzini
   It will prove of interest to the priest and seminarian as well as to the lay intellectual seeking a deeper penetration into moral law. 240 pages
cloth $4.00 — RA0110

God and the Problem of Evil
Sr. Concetta Belleggia, D.S.P.
   Is God the inventor of evil or is man?
   In answering for everyone this age-old question, this book treats the problem of evil in terms of its nature, its causes and its relationship to God, as these have been analyzed and investigated in the writings of Jacques Maritain, who, in turn, seeks his own support in the treatment offered by St. Thomas. 122 pages
cloth $3.75; paper $2.50 — RA0113

God Is Alive
Daughters of St. Paul
Key truths of the Catholic Faith.
6¢ — PM0810

The Human Knowledge of Christ
Rev. Bertrand de Margerie, S.J.
   In this book a noted theologian takes up the principal objections to the traditional teaching of the Church concerning the human knowledge of Christ and shows how these present accusations lack consistency. 80 pages
cloth $2.95; paper $1.50 — SC0055

Human Life is Sacred
Irish Bishops' Pastoral on
   Abortion
   Euthanasia
   Human Sexuality
   Contraception
(With study guidelines.)
   With warm style, this pastoral

letter deals with one of the main topics of our time. People have always discussed sex, marriage, human dignity and violence but never as openly and as continuously as now. Faced with this non-stop public debate, the Christian may wonder what his religion has to offer. This pastoral letter gives the answer clearly: Human life *is* sacred. 79 pages
paper $1.50 — MS0300

In Defense of Life
Most Rev. John J. O'Connor

Is it possible to have a just war today? Can the use of nuclear weapons ever be justified? Is conscientious objection a right, a duty, neither, or both? This book attempts to reply to these questions in the light of the official teaching of the Church. 140 pages
cloth $4.00; paper $3.00 — RA0117

Living the Catholic Faith Today
Most Rev. John F. Whealon, STD, SSL, DD

This short volume packs a wealth of insights on practicing the Catholic faith now. Among many topics—Why believe in God; Why be a Roman Catholic; Ideas on parish life; Practial Ideas on Confession; How should a Catholic live the faith. A book to be owned by every Catholic adult and inquirer into the faith.
130 pages
cloth $2.50; paper $1.50 — RA0130

The Lord of History
Msgr. Eugene Kevane

"This is an excellent introduction to the Christian philosophy of history—clearly written, comprehensive within the limits of its less than 200 pages, and cognizant of the important modern issues." (From a review by James Hitchcock, Fellowship of Catholic Scholars) 200 pages
cloth $4.00; paper $3.00 — RA0135

The Many Whys of Life
Rev. Joseph McCarthy

A book chock-full of thoughts—thoughts and answers for men and women besieged by a deluge of questions. 246 pages
cloth $3.00; paper $2.00 — RA0140

Religion for People of Today
Daughters of St. Paul

Squarely facing the questions everyone is asking in these days of confusion, this concise religious instruction book speaks modern man's language. Solid in its doctrine, contemporary in its presentation, it will prove ideal for adult discussion groups, classes or individual reading.
112 pages
Magister paperback $1.25 — RA0150

Remarried Divorcees and Eucharistic Communion
Rev. Bertrand de Margerie, S.J.

This book examines the problem from a solid scriptural basis, within the context of both the Old and New Testaments, and traces the clear and unbroken line of doctrinal teaching on this subject down the centuries, from the Fathers of the Church to post-Tridentine theologians. 112 pages
cloth $3.00; paper $1.95 — MS0593

Rite of Penance (Leaflet)

Concise, easy-to-follow leaflet on the new rite of Penance which includes the choice of responses for the penitent. This inexpensive leaflet is a welcome aid to priests and laity alike in the celebration of the sacrament of forgiveness.
4 pages; 6¢ — MS0610

Sexual Inversion: The Questions—With Catholic Answers

Rev. Herbert F. Smith, S.J., with Joseph A. Di Ienno, M.D. Introduction by V. Michael Vaccaro, M.D.

Informative treatment of such topics as: Homosexuality, morality, and religion; homosexuality and the medical sciences; homosexuality and society; living with one's homosexual orientation.
cloth $2.95; paper $1.95 — RA0165

Symposium on the Magisterium: A Positive Statement

Edited by Msgr. John J. O'Rourke and S. Thomas Greenburg

A positive response to the continuing debate about the Magisterium, its meaning, composition, authority and proper function. Among those taking part in the symposium were Cardinal Krol of Philadelphia, Archbishop Whealon of Hartford, Bishop Maloney, Abbot McCaffrey, and others. 152 pages
cloth $5.95; paper $4.50 — RA0185

The Ten Commandments

Daughters of St. Paul

Ideal for use in preparation for the sacrament of Reconciliation, this pamphlet provides questions and answers that serve as a basis for personal examination of conscience on the Commandments of God. 14 pages
15¢ — PM1909

Visible Community of Love

Daughters of St. Paul

A dynamic comparative religions source that sets forth the living Church in action—dialoguing with atheists, Jews, Moslems, Buddhists and non-Catholic Christians. Moving photos and sayings by famous spiritual writers throughout. 240 pages
cloth $5.00; paper $4.00 — CA0160

"What Think You of Christ?"

R.M. Levy

"This book can be called God's revelation to the human race as seen through the one who has looked for the face of God and somehow is beginning to find it." "Franciscan Message" 102 pages
cloth $1.50 — RA0200

Why a Gift on Sunday?

Rev. John M. Scott, S.J.

"Why go to Mass?" In an effort to catch the wonder and fascination of what has been called "the most beautiful thing this side of heaven," the author provides compelling reasons and insights. The Mass is our gift to God and His gift to us. 148 pages
cloth $2.95; paper $1.95 — RA0210

Please order from addresses on the following page, specifying title and item number.

Daughters of St. Paul

IN MASSACHUSETTS
  50 St. Paul's Ave., Jamaica Plain, Boston, MA 02130;
    617-522-8911; 617-522-0875
  172 Tremont Street, Boston, MA 02111; 617-426-5464;
    617-426-4230
IN NEW YORK
  78 Fort Place, Staten Island, NY 10301; 212-447-5071
  59 East 43rd Street, New York, NY 10017; 212-986-7580
  625 East 187th Street, Bronx, NY 10458; 212-584-0440
  525 Main Street, Buffalo, NY 14203; 716-847-6044
IN NEW JERSEY
  Hudson Mall — Route 440 and Communipaw Ave.,
    Jersey City, NJ 07304; 201-433-7740
IN CONNECTICUT
  202 Fairfield Ave., Bridgeport, CT 06604; 203-335-9913
IN OHIO
  2105 Ontario St. (at Prospect Ave.), Cleveland, OH 44115; 216-621-9427
  25 E. Eighth Street, Cincinnati, OH 45202; 513-721-4838
IN PENNSYLVANIA
  1719 Chestnut Street, Philadelphia, PA 19103; 215-568-2638
IN VIRGINIA
  1025 King St., Alexandria, VA 22314 703-683-1741
IN FLORIDA
  2700 Biscayne Blvd., Miami, FL 33137; 305-573-1618
IN LOUISIANA
  4403 Veterans Memorial Blvd., Metairie, LA 70002; 504-887-7631;
    504-887-0113
  1800 South Acadian Thruway, P.O. Box 2028, Baton Rouge, LA 70821
    504-343-4057; 504-343-3814
IN MISSOURI
  1001 Pine Street (at North 10th), St. Louis, MO 63101; 314-621-0346;
    314-231-1034
IN ILLINOIS
  172 North Michigan Ave., Chicago, IL 60601; 312-346-4228
    312-346-3240
IN TEXAS
  114 Main Plaza, San Antonio, TX 78205; 512-224-8101
IN CALIFORNIA
  1570 Fifth Avenue, San Diego, CA 92101; 714-232-1442
  46 Geary Street, San Francisco, CA 94108; 415-781-5180
IN HAWAII
  1143 Bishop Street, Honolulu, HI 96813; 808-521-2731
IN ALASKA
  750 West 5th Avenue, Anchorage AK 99501; 907-272-8183
IN CANADA
  3022 Dufferin Street, Toronto 395, Ontario, Canada
IN ENGLAND
  128, Notting Hill Gate, London W11 3QG, England
  133 Corporation Street, Birmingham B4 6PH, England
  5A-7 Royal Exchange Square, Glasgow G1 3AH, England
  82 Bold Street, Liverpool L1 4HR, England
IN AUSTRALIA
  58 Abbotsford Rd., Homebush, N.S.W., Sydney 2140, Australia